Frances K. Grossman
Alexandra B. Cook
Selin S. Kepkep
Karestan C. Koenen

With the Phoenix Rising

Lessons from Ten Resilient Women Who Overcame the Trauma of Childhood Sexual Abuse

Jossey-Bass Publishers
San Francisco

Jossey-Bass books and products are available through most bookstores. To contact Jossey-Bass directly, call (888) 378-2537, fax to (800) 605-2665, or visit our website at www.josseybass.com.

Substantial discounts on bulk quantities of Jossey-Bass books are available to corporations, professional associations, and other organizations. For details and discount information, contact the special sales department at Jossey-Bass.

 Manufactured in the United States of America on Lyons Falls Turin Book. This paper is acid-free and 100 percent totally chlorine-free.

Library of Congress Cataloging-in-Publication Data

With the phoenix rising : lessons from ten resilient women who
overcame the trauma of childhood sexual abuse / Frances K. Grossman
. . . [et al.]. — 1st ed.
      p.   cm.
   Includes bibliographical references and index.
   ISBN 0-7879-4784-9 (alk. paper)
   1. Adult child sexual abuse victims—Case studies.   I. Grossman,
Frances Kaplan, date.
RC569.5.A28 W57 1999
616.85'8369—dc21   98-58-064

FIRST EDITION
HB Printing   10 9 8 7 6 5 4 3 2 1

Contents

Part IV: A Lifelong Process

Preface

The phoenix in our title is a beautiful bird described in Egyptian mythology that lived for five hundred years, was consumed in fire, and then rose anew from the ashes. Resilient survivors of serious childhood sexual abuse have been, in important ways, consumed by the destructive power of the horrors visited upon them and then have reconstructed themselves out of the ashes. This book grew out of our interest in learning more about how people do that—about what allows children and adults to do well in the world in spite of their horrific life experiences. As psychologists, we are often asked to focus on what is wrong with someone and how that came to be. Yet sometimes people show enormous strength when we might have expected them to fail. How does this happen? If we can understand something about how it happens and what contributes to that process, perhaps we can help those who are less fortunate by engendering the same processes in them.

Doing well in the face of difficult life circumstances is called resiliency. Some people believe that resiliency is based primarily on genetic factors such as intelligence, temperament, or strength of character. Others believe it is more affected by factors in the environment such as secure parental relationships, positive school experiences, and healthy peer relationships. Most researchers assume that resiliency is composed of some complicated combination of factors.

In this book we focus on resiliency in a particular group—women with histories of severe, usually incestuous, sexual abuse. Although at times we talk generally about resilient adaptation, our focus is on resilient responses to childhood sexual trauma.

We—a group of clinical psychologists who are also psychotherapists—were interested in hearing what survivors think contributed to their resiliency. Survivors, to us, are people who have experienced serious childhood sexual abuse and yet have found ways to continue to live in the world, to love, and to work. We spoke at length during a period of eight years with ten women who had experienced severe childhood sexual abuse. We then analyzed those interviews using qualitative research methods. This book reflects these women's voices and our own understanding, which is based on an integration of what they told us, what we know from the literature, and what we know from our experiences with clients. We hope this work will help therapists shift the focus from vulnerabilities to strengths in their work with survivors of abuse. Survivors themselves can benefit greatly from understanding what helps someone succeed rather than fail.

ORGANIZATION OF THE BOOK

The chapters are grouped into four major sections. In Part One we lay the groundwork for later discussions by reviewing the literature, briefly describing what we did in the study, and introducing our participants. In Part Two we explore what our participants told us about their resiliency within a variety of contexts and draw out the implications for therapy with survivors. In Part Three we highlight the important processes that influenced these women's ability to succeed and how this information can be applied by therapists. Last, in Part Four we describe our follow-up interviews with the participants; they summarize what happened in their lives in the five to eight intervening years, and we suggest what can be learned from their stories.

In Chapter One we give a brief history of the concept of resiliency as other researchers and theorists have understood it. We then describe our views of resiliency and how they influence the subsequent chapters. In Chapter Two we introduce the reader to our ten participants through a brief synopsis of their lives.

In Part Two we focus on some of the most important contexts of our participants' lives, the ways they manifest their resiliency in those environments, and what implications this information might have for therapists working with similar clients. Chapter Three describes how, for most of our participants, school and work have been safe havens, providing opportunities to thrive and accomplish and to have good relationships with friends and teachers. In Chapters Four and Five we turn to participants' current family situations and focus first on the strengths manifest in their relationships with intimate partners and then on their resiliency in their connections with their children. In Chapter Six we explore aspects of our participants' relationships with other people, pets, and things.

In Part Three we address some larger processes and strategies these women used that might help others develop resiliency. In Chapter Seven we concentrate on the role that psychotherapy, in its variety of forms, has played in the women's recovery; we then explore some of the particularly important therapeutic processes they described. In Chapter Eight we examine how the participants managed their feelings in childhood and adulthood. The process of taking care of oneself through setting boundaries, using coping strategies, and looking out for one's mind and body is a cornerstone of resiliency and is the focus of Chapter Nine. In Chapter Ten we describe how the participants made sense of their abuse and how, as adults, they have often used that experience to find ways to help other people.

Part Four offers a particularly rich and unique perspective. After years of analyzing the participants' interview transcripts and of writing the chapters just described, we met again with each of the women to hear what had happened in the intervening period and to give them an opportunity to respond to what we had written about them. In the final chapter we discuss the implications of their thoughtful and hopeful comments for all therapists working with abuse survivors.

In our clinical opinion, most survivors of serious abuse or neglect could benefit from a long-term therapeutic relationship. Unfortunately, in these times of managed care, this treatment modality is not available to all, or even most, clients. We believe our emphasis on survivors' strengths, as well as their vulnerabilities, can be particularly useful to therapists and their clients and that many of the recommendations we make here can be usefully applied in managed care settings. Therapists operating under such constraints must teach their trauma clients to identify and use their own inner and outer resources rather than focus on their own psychopathology. Brief therapy can be used to sow the seeds of this new perspective, and an intermittent therapy model (not uncommon with managed care) can be used to nurture the growth of this new perspective.

ACKNOWLEDGMENTS

Many people, over a number of years, have made substantial contributions to this book. One crucial group is made up of the women who courageously shared their histories with us. The other group is made up of all those who were, at one time or another, members of the Boston University Resiliency Project (affectionately called BURP) with the Department of Psychology at Boston University. Several worked on the project for a number of years and made substantial contributions, even though their life circumstances did not permit them to participate in the final stage of writing the book. We want to acknowledge those women: Katharine Culhane, Lou-Marie Kruger, Judy Lam, Roslin P. Moore, and Rhea Paniesin; Judy gave us important comments on a draft of the manuscript and made many other contributions. Others who contributed their time, energy, good ideas, and enthusiasm to the research group were Cheryl Baresi, Ruth

Bell, Antonia Bookbinder, Karen Curto, Colleen Gregory, Kerry Gruber, Judith Jordan, Jodi Kilgannon, Stephanie Marcy, Guerda Nicholas, Debra Reuben, Liesl Rockhart, Nurit Scheinberg, Etay Shilony, Sharon Thrasher, Bradford Stolback, Anne Watkins, and Claudia Yellin. We are indebted to Kari A. Gleiser, who came up with the powerful image of the phoenix for the title.

Catherine Jacobus and Hank Grossman did a wonderful job of going over the manuscript with a fine-toothed comb and helping us say what we wanted to say more clearly.

The Department of Psychology at Boston University provided endless reams of paper, as well as the strong support staff essential for such a project. In particular, Fabio Idrobe was amazing in helping us master the computer program "HyperRESEARCH" and debugging the computer when it balked frequently at the huge amounts of information we were asking it to process. Jeff Gagne was always friendly and helpful, as he made thousands of copies of measures, minutes of research meetings, transcripts of interviews, and drafts of chapters.

Finally, in this day of lean budgets for presses, with little to spare to help authors polish manuscripts, we feel incredibly fortunate to have found an editor, Leslie Berriman at Jossey-Bass, who had the vision to see what the book could be and the wonderful commitment and skills to provide the editorial assistance we had longed for and desperately needed.

March 1999

Frances K. Grossman
Boston

Alexandra B. Cook
Boston

Selin S. Kepkep
Boston

Karestan C. Koenen
New York

We want to thank members of our families,
who contributed in many ways, according to their ages
and stages, but always with love:
Hank, Jenny, and Benj Grossman
John and David Conforti, Catherine Jacobus
Brad and Jacob Kaya Kepkep Harris, Pat and Cevat Kepkep
Austin and Kathleen Koenen, David Soliz

With the Phoenix Rising

Part I

Setting the Stage

1

Resiliency

We all know people who have undergone terrible experiences in childhood and yet find ways to love and work with talent and enthusiasm—to live fully and sometimes even joyfully. We call them resilient. We know others who are so damaged by what has happened to them that they are crippled by symptoms or lose their enthusiasm for life and relationships. When we look more closely at people in both groups, we are likely to see many who had difficult childhood experiences but are doing well in some ways, perhaps not so well in others.

We believe that therapists who work with survivors of childhood trauma have much to learn from studying individuals who show resiliency in some aspect of their lives. This book is about what we, as clinicians and researchers, have learned about resiliency from ten women who were courageous enough to share their stories with us. We believe that their stories contain helpful lessons for clinicians about ways to notice and nurture resiliency in their own clients who have survived traumatic childhoods. We begin this chapter with a discussion of what others have thought

---

Note: This chapter was authored by the following, in the order listed: J. N. Lam, F. K. Grossman, A. B. Cook, S. S. Kepkep, K. Culhane, R. P. Moore, R. Paniesin, and K. C. Koenen.

and said about resiliency, concluding with a brief overview of the lenses we have found helpful.

WHAT IS RESILIENCY?

Resiliency has been defined as doing well in the face of a history of serious stress or trauma, which is generally the way we use the term here. But resiliency is not a new topic. Even before it became a subject for research, many clinicians were impressed by the number of individuals who showed considerable strength, even though they had experienced terrible life events. How is this possible? How do they do it? From our years of treating and researching trauma, we know that some people with histories of serious childhood sexual abuse do indeed show long-lasting negative effects. Yet a surprisingly large number seem to do just fine. Studies have shown that as many as half of those with histories of serious childhood sexual abuse do not show measurable psychological symptoms (Herman, Russell, & Trocki, 1986).

Interest in the idea of resiliency did not begin with a focus on childhood abuse but on children of parents with mental illness and on poverty-stricken children. Originally, these children were thought of as superkids—children who showed no apparent ill effects of adversity (Kaufman, Grunebaum, Cohler, & Gamer, 1979). A literature emerged around the idea that some children were invulnerable to the effects of a variety of stress factors, including maltreatment and trauma. This type of resilience was typically measured by the absence of psychopathology, by good school achievement, and by high overall intellectual functioning. Although this original research was groundbreaking in its focus on health instead of pathology, it was simplistic in that resiliency in these children was categorized as present or absent rather than as lying along a continuum. The research has since progressed to a more complex understanding of what contributes to resiliency and vulnerability.

THE RESEARCH ON RESILIENCY

In the 1970s a British research psychiatrist, Michael Rutter, was studying the role of what he called *risk factors* in how children managed in their lives (see Rutter, 1985, 1987). What he meant by *risk* was important life experiences or situations that we know can be detrimental to children's development. He looked at such factors as mental illness or alcoholism in a parent, extreme poverty, or foster home placement for the child. He found that having one serious risk factor did not increase the likelihood that a child would develop mental illness, a conduct disorder, or a learning difficulty. However, having two of these risk factors greatly increased the chance that the child would run into difficulty at some point; three risk factors made it ten times more likely.

Rutter also noted that some children with two or more serious risk factors did not run into trouble in obvious ways, and he described these children as resilient. He was curious about them and began to study whether there were positive factors or resources in their lives that buffered them, to some degree, from the negative effects of risk. He called these positive resources *protective factors* and found that resilient children tended to have more of them than less resilient children. As he and other researchers (for example, Garmezy, 1993; Werner & Smith, 1979) began to explore protective factors, they found these clustered into three different categories: those in the individual child, those in the family, and those in the community. Protective factors in the child included such things as being born with a positive temperament or high intelligence. Family factors included a good relationship with at least one parent, family warmth, and good communication between the parents. Finally, protective factors in the larger community included such dimensions as an organized, coherent neighborhood.

As Rutter and others carried out research on resiliency, they struggled to define precisely what they meant by the term, and we have continued that struggle. The concept gets more elusive the more closely it is examined. For example, how can we compare the resiliency of two children, both doing equally well, one with a history of terrible life circumstances and the other with some stress in her history but not serious trauma? Are they both resilient—or only the one with a terrible history? Or when we compare two adults who seem to be doing equally well—both of whom have histories of severe abuse but one of whom had a strong relationship with his mother throughout his childhood—can we infer that the one without the strong protective factor is more resilient?

Let us illustrate another common set of issues in understanding resiliency. How do we evaluate a woman who has a history of serious trauma, who is doing extremely well in work, but whose relationships are difficult and limited? Is she resilient? Or at the extreme, what about the child who has grown up with a psychotic parent in a completely disorganized and toxic environment, has a major mental illness, has been hospitalized off and on, but has been able to maintain some family ties and is not homeless or dead? Could we call his adaptation resilient, as compared with someone else with a similar history? Is labeling someone *resilient* saying anything more than that she has undergone some hardship and is doing well in some arena that we chose to examine?

For these and other reasons, the term has continued to elude a definition that most researchers can accept and that can be translated into concrete terms. Rutter, for example, considered a child to be resilient who, in the face of two or more serious risk factors, did not show evident mental illness, was not considered a juvenile delinquent by the law, and did not have major difficulty learning in school. Two psychoanalytic researchers, Murphy and Moriarity (1976), viewed resilience as a child's capacity to recover from what they referred to as "disturbances in equilibrium," or what is now more commonly understood as severe stress, such as the death of a parent, family mental illness, or extensive physical injury resulting from a serious accident.

In a longitudinal study of Harvard men, Felsman and Vaillant (1987) describe a different kind of strength that they believe under-lies resiliency. Generally, these men were highly favored in their lives, but some had suffered difficult and at times traumatic experiences; not all ended up doing well, either by their own or others' accounts. Felsman and Vaillant were struck by the fact that men who had experienced very difficult life events and had done well anyway had "access to their pasts and are able to bear that pain and sorrow, and in so doing, to draw upon it as a source of strength" (p. 55). Thus they found that the resilient men's capacity to ac-knowledge and remember stressful or traumatic life experiences with feeling and understanding distinguished them from their less re-silient peers. This perspective is consistent with much of the liter-ature on healing from trauma, and it emphasizes that people need to acknowledge and remember traumatic events in order to be re-leased from the hold such events can have on their lives.

In the past fifteen years, clinicians and a few researchers have begun to focus more specifically on resiliency in individuals with his-tories of childhood sexual abuse. For example, in one study Mrazek and Mrazek (1987) found that personal characteristics and skills greatly influence a traumatized child's resiliency—characteristics that are influenced by genetics and positive life circumstances such as hav-ing middle- or upper-class economic status, educated parents, a sup-portive family, a supportive social network and community services, and an adult mentor. But the researchers make an important point: characteristics that can help protect a child from the impact of abuse, such as precocious maturity, are not necessarily positive or desirable. Although it may be essential to a child while the trauma is occurring, it could well hinder development in adolescence, when an important task is to solidify peer relationships. Furthermore, how these protec-tive factors influence a child's functioning can change with time.

Mrazek and Mrazek argue further that events or characteristics traditionally regarded as risk factors can function as protective fac-tors, depending on the circumstances. For example, placement in a foster home is generally considered a strong risk factor, but placement that takes a child out of an abusive family can be a protective factor as well. Finally, these researchers talk about the abuse and the context immediately surrounding it, which can be more or less protective. An offender's rapid acknowledgment of the abuse, a nonabusive parent's full support, the child's feeling of being validated in a therapeutic context, the child's custody resolved, or placement in a competent foster home can serve to protect the child from what might otherwise be a much more negative effect of trauma.

Another line of research in resiliency has focused on the aspects of individuals' thinking that psychologists call cognitive processes (for example, Taylor, 1983; Janoff-Bulman, 1992). We know that most of the negative effects of abuse involve changes in the way people view themselves and the world. Specifically, their sense of safety in the world and trust in other people has been destroyed. They often see themselves as responsible for the abuse, yet they are paralyzed when it comes to taking steps to protect themselves. Moreover, as Lisa McCann and Laurie Pearlman (1993) suggest, survivors often go through an existential crisis, asking, Why did this happen to me? Thus an important aspect of recovery involves finding a way to think about traumatic experiences that allows the survivor to participate fully and meaningfully in life by regaining a realistic sense of safety and trust. Judith Herman (1992) believes an essential part of later-stage recovery is finding a way to make meaning of the trauma by taking social or political action, such as influencing public policy or helping other survivors.

Ann Masten and Douglas Coatsworth (1998) have written about the "foundations of competence," which they see as central to resilient adaptation. In reviewing the literature, they highlight some important issues. First of all, they note that "resilient children do not appear to possess mysterious or unique qualities; rather, they have retained or secured important resources representing basic protective systems in human development" (p. 212). Second, based on some research findings, they raise the question of whether resilient children actually feel more distress because of their competence. We wonder if these children have the internal strength necessary to bear more pain, as opposed to having to invoke primitive defenses to manage that pain. Another hypothesis might be that because these children and adults look strong, more is expected of them and their internal suffering is less likely to be acknowledged or tolerated. Last, Masten and Coatsworth point out that a global concept of resiliency is not as useful as an appreciation of multiple domains of both competence and risk.

OUR UNDERSTANDING OF RESILIENCY

On the basis of the literature we have outlined, our many collective years of experience researching resilient adolescents and adults, and our clinical work with survivors who are resilient to varying degrees, we have come to the way of thinking about the concept that informs this book. Our understanding and its implications are described in the remainder of the chapter.

The Importance of Context

Risk and resiliency occur in a context, that is, with one or more events happening to a particular individual in a specific family and neighborhood. For example, the consequences of risk or trauma in a person's life are, in crucial ways, influenced by the type, intensity, and duration of the event or set of events. These and other specifics provide the backdrop of risk and resilience. We are convinced, as are others (for example, Harvey, 1996; Lyons, 1991) that resilience can only be understood with those particulars in mind. For example, all rapes are not the same and do not have the same impact. The rape of an adolescent by a date is very different psychologically from the rape of a two-year-old by her father, even though both are serious assaults and can have powerful negative effects. Further, the characteristics of the person to whom these assaults happen greatly influence her response, as do the responses of important people around her at the time of the event. At the very least, then, a consideration of contextual factors should include knowledge of the specific nature, timing, and meaning of the trauma.

People's lives, mental and physical, are embedded in families and communities. Therefore all aspects of mind, body, and environment influence the impact of trauma (see van der Kolk, McFarlane, & Weisaeth, 1996). An individual has inborn resources or traits that are encouraged or discouraged by familial and social environments, and this interaction influences her thoughts, feelings, and behaviors. Moreover, environmental factors such as parenting have a different impact under different socioeconomic conditions (Baldwin, Baldwin, Kesser, Zax, Sameroff, & Seifer, 1993). Specifically, effective parenting under advantageous circumstances is not the same as effective parenting under financial and social stress. Research continues to support the relatively equal impact of individual child factors such as intelligence, locus of control, and temperament, as well as environmental factors such as parental attachment, family structure, and effective schooling (reviewed in Masten & Coatsworth, 1998). All of these differences influence the quality of experiences, how they are interpreted, and the resulting effects on the individual.

In this study, context has been the factor that has influenced us most. Its importance is reflected in our commitment to studying a diverse sample of women. The context of their lives varied considerably. Context was also central in our decision to use a qualitative research method. This approach—paying close attention to the words and stories of each participant—was developed in large part to preserve the context of people's lives. One example from our research was that the two African American women in our sample grew up with the particular strengths that were related to the family style of urban, black families. Even in the context of abusive families, they learned early, from their mother and others, that it was appropriate and necessary for them to take care of themselves. This was a different lesson from the one many girls in abusive white families learned: that it was wrong and selfish to protect or defend themselves and that girls and women did not do that.

Life Span Development

Any understanding of resilience must take into account what psychologists call a life span developmental perspective—a view that emphasizes change over time as individuals grow and evolve. In other words, an event that occurs at one time in a person's life would have a different effect at another time. One important implication of this approach is that traumatic events do not present a person with a single coping task but with a series of tasks at different stages, each stage to be examined separately (Newberger & de Vos, 1988). For example, a young child who must cope effectively with incestuous abuse requires particular strengths or abilities. Thus, dissociating from sexual trauma in the moment may be the only active coping strategy available to the child and is an effective way to manage her overwhelming experience. But when that child is an adult and faces first-time parenthood, the challenge demands a different response. Dissociation at this stage is not adaptive, for it would put mother and child at risk. The new baby will trigger old emotions, but the mother's task is to stay in the present, face the anxieties and stresses of labor and delivery, and then deal with the lingering aftermath of trauma.

Furthermore, a survivor's success in coping with one task does not guarantee her ability to cope well with other tasks at the same or different times. Among the variables is the availability of strong supports. For example, her mother as the primary caretaker may have been unable to acknowledge the early abuse at all, but years later she may be supportive around childbirth and early parenting. Moreover, the survivor may well have the support of friends and a spouse in adulthood, in contrast to the isolation of her youth.

Consequently, an individual's resilience in the face of stress changes throughout development and sometimes reflects itself in what appears to be disrupted or even psychopathological behavior. But even such low points as bouts of depression and subsequent hospitalizations, which are usually viewed as manifestations of mental illness, may be understood as resiliency. They can provide opportunities for fruitful therapeutic and developmental work. The context and timing of these apparent breakdowns must influence our view of whether or not they represent resilient behavior, in whole or in part.

Sometimes, coping with stressful events can increase resilient children's future coping resources because they develop confidence in their ability. However, strategies that children use to cope with abuse can become maladaptive if not transformed later in life. These factors can be particularly problematic if they become fixated and are used inappropriately or indiscriminately later in life. For example, the use of dissociation at certain times during abusive episodes in childhood might be extremely helpful, but this same response to adult stress can make the development of intimate relationships difficult or impossible. What might appear at the time to be good adaptation, such as freedom from extreme emotional distress, may not be helpful or even desirable in the long run. Early resilience may be bought at the cost of later spontaneity or flexibility.

In thinking about the later years of the life span, it is clear that the demands of aging often interact with early risk or trauma to determine current levels of functioning. For example, one researcher has found that Holocaust survivors are often more vulnerable to subsequent stresses such as difficulties in meeting the demands of aging (Danieli, 1994a, 1994b). Others have found that people who have encountered early, serious adversity may experience an increased severity of posttraumatic stress disorder (PTSD) symptoms later in life because of additional stressors, losses, or failing health (see, for example, Yehuda, Kahana, Schmeidler, Steven, et al., 1995). However, there is also evidence that resilience is a capacity that can increase over time.

Psychologist Gina O'Connell Higgins found that the resilient individuals she studied who had experienced terrible childhoods with repeated childhood physical or sexual abuse did not evidence a decline in their resilience (Higgins, 1994). She notes that many of her research participants would not have appeared resilient at earlier stages in their lives, but they were over forty when she interviewed them. All were in committed, ten- to fifteen-year relationships and were many years away from their painful childhood experiences. We wonder if people whose resilience declines continue to be exposed to unusually stressful life circumstances, whereas the participants in Higgins's study were not. This raises the questions: How are some individuals able to remove themselves from adverse circumstances and others are not? and How much relates to real-life issues like economic resources? For some people, resilience may increase developmentally and in some way depend on the maturity that comes only with age.

We were particularly interested in comparing what our participants told us about their resiliency in childhood with their observations about their strengths at the time of the interviews many years later. To give one example, we saw clearly how our participants recalled their childhood limitations in managing their intense and difficult feelings, and how many more options they had in adulthood. And again we saw, as other clinicians and researchers have seen, that in a survivor's adaptation, a period of intense distress and apparent deterioration, even severe enough to require hospitalization, is not necessarily a negative factor in the long term. For our participants, such episodes sometimes represented clear and positive turning points, even if the events were experienced as destructive at the time.

Our good fortune in being able to interview all ten women at the follow-up five to eight years later adds an important longitudinal look at resiliency. We were awed by the degree of positive change we saw in these women and by the fact that we saw it in every single woman in the study.

MULTIDIMENSIONAL DOMAINS

We believe that any definition of resiliency must be multidimensional. Simple, single definitions work only in a limited way. For example, the question, Is this individual resilient?, is devoid of context. To be meaningful, it must be made much more specific and relate to events and standards. Is this person resilient with respect to this event, this context, or to that standard? If we are interested in how well a survivor is doing with respect to work or school, then we need to define resiliency with regard to doing well in those contexts. However, if we are primarily interested in the quality of personal relationships or the amount of psychological pain, we will have different ways of defining resiliency. Depending on the different definitions, different people can appear to be resilient. Resiliency in one arena of life does not ensure resiliency in all other domains. Viewing resiliency from many perspectives can be helpful in understanding what individuals or groups need.

Our participants had some areas of clear and impressive resiliency and others in which they continued to struggle. It was never possible for us to say, "This person is resilient" or "That participant is not resilient." Statements we *can* feel comfortable making are "This individual is exceedingly resilient in her ability to develop enduring and supportive friendships," and "This woman is particularly vulnerable, and not very resilient, in her continuing inability to find healthy ways of soothing herself in the face of experiences of loss."

RESILIENT PROCESSES
AND CHARACTERISTICS

Some definitions of resiliency have focused on processes, whereas others have focused on characteristics of the individual. Processes can be thought of as ways of going about the business of dealing with life events. Examples of processes are a survivor's efforts to make sense of why the trauma happened to her or a survivor's ways of coping with trauma-related painful feelings when they arise. Mary Harvey (1996, p. 34) talks about a number of resiliency-related processes: having authority over memory (the choice of thinking about events versus not being able to remember or their unbidden intrusion), integration of emotion and memory, tolerance for strong feelings, mastery over symptoms, the ability to make safe attachment relationships, and the capacity to find meaning in the trauma. We agree with Michael Rutter (1987) who said, "Protection does not reside in the psychological chemistry of the moment but the ways in which people deal with life changes and in what they do about their stressful or disadvantageous circumstances" (p. 329). Many people have a strong need or drive to be integrated, to be whole. When their wholeness is disrupted by trauma, they continue to struggle to find ways to regain their integrated selfhood and often use all resources available to them. That struggle is represented by processes.

In contrast, characteristics are traits that tend to be stable in a person's life, such as a general tendency to believe that one's own actions are the strongest influence on what happens to one or the trait of high intelligence. We believe that any definition of resiliency must consider both processes and characteristics. In this project we look at both perspectives.

Furthermore, resilient processes or characteristics are often not inherently good or bad, although they can be very useful at a particular time in a survivor's life. Some of the abilities that further the functioning of resilient individuals in some areas can, at the same time, interfere with how they are doing in others. For example, a survivor may be functioning well in work or school, partly because he is driven and perfectionistic. But in another area, such as parenting, which requires a very different set of abilities, his perfectionism may be detrimental (Wortman, 1983).

Like many other researchers, we did find resilient characteristics that were helpful to some of our participants, such as particular intelligence or an early tendency to be independent, which allowed them to move away from their abusive families earlier than others might.

Thought Processes

We know that cognitive responses—the way people think—greatly influence people's response to stress and trauma. People who think positively about life events generally do better over time. Traumatic experiences tend to cause people to view the world negatively, to emphasize unfairness and malevolence, to focus on their own vulnerability, and to doubt that they deserve to be treated fairly. Janoff-Bulman (1989) argues that, for many traumatized individuals, a central cognitive task is to find a way to understand what happened to them so they can hold a more balanced view of themselves and their world. Resiliency requires survivors to find a way to include both the good and the bad in their view of the world, in order to reduce their sensitivity to risk and regain their sense of safety.

Finding or making meaning is a crucially important process in survivors' resiliency. The knowledge and feelings experienced in the trauma have to be absorbed and processed by the individual, who then must find some way to make sense of the experience. On the one hand, survivors who can do that successfully feel less guilt and isolation than those who cannot; on the other hand, as Silver, Boon, and Stone (1983) found, it is counterproductive to continue to search for meaning without ever arriving at some sense of understanding and closure.

Self-understanding, which is one aspect of meaning making, fosters resilience because it provides a way of making sense of what has occurred. According to psychiatrist William Beardslee (1989), who takes a developmental stance toward resiliency, there are five dimensions to self-understanding. First, resilient individuals can think more clearly about what they are trying to understand. Second, they can figure out what actions are possible and what will be the likely consequences of those actions, such as getting married or divorced, starting or leaving therapy, or having or adopting a child. Third, the actions they take are based on an understanding of what happened and why. They wish to act on their knowledge and experience, particularly by helping others in some way. Fourth, as these resilient individuals age and mature, their understanding changes, deepens, and becomes more comprehensive. When they themselves become parents, for example, their understanding of their own parents must continue to deepen. Fifth, the self-understanding they develop helps them cope with other stresses and promotes further resilience. For Beardslee, such self-understanding implies not just thought but the active participation of the individual in the world. An example might be a survivor whose self-awareness prompts him to get involved in educating others about child abuse.

Also, resilience can be conceptualized as the ability to recover from trauma cognitively and emotionally. While a traumatic event is happening, most people's ability to think is limited by a variety of protective mechanisms such as massive or partial repression, dissociation, and intellectualization. During recovery, it is possible to gauge resiliency in the way people use such processes as compartmentalizing their feelings (for instance limiting their intense distress to the therapy session and to the privacy of their own home), coming to a different understanding of the events, being flexible in the way they think of themselves and others, and learning new ways to nurture and satisfy themselves. Moreover, the ability to tolerate arousal and emotional distress, to rework and reappraise the powerful "new" data, and to obtain or accept the support of others are three important factors that can be regarded as crucial capacities underlying resilience.

Although we knew about the long history of research on cognition, we were still surprised at how central the role of thinking was to our participants' healing. They all told us how they had learned to change destructive ways of thinking about themselves and their histories and had learned to control their thinking in ways that greatly contributed to their resilient adaptation. Clearly, psychotherapy played a major role in teaching them about this, but for many it was not the only source of their learning. Because thinking is such a powerful tool for adult survivors, we are struck by the difficulty that child survivors, whose cognitive abilities are more limited, have in coping with their traumatic experiences.

Making sense of their histories is a central task for survivors, whether they conclude that there is no sense to be made, that the abuse was just a random event in the world, or that the abuse is a consequence of many generations of family history. Important findings from our study were the extent to which altruistic behavior was a consequence of the sense many of our participants made of their histories as well as the many ways these women were contributing to their friends and communities.

Tolerance of Emotional Distress

As the example of Holocaust survivors who successfully established careers but were less able to manage close relationships illustrates, individuals can be successful in many areas of their lives but still suffer significant emotional distress. The research literature has generally considered individuals resilient if they do not develop signs of psychopathology or marked distress following disastrous experiences. For example, in research as in life, children are generally considered resilient if they are able to return to the level of functioning they showed before a traumatic or stressful event. However, signs of emotional distress such as depression, anxiety, or PTSD are not necessarily evidence of a lack of resilience. Conversely, the absence of symptoms may not necessarily be a sign of resilience. As too little of the literature acknowledges, resilient individuals often continue to make use of their resources and strengths and to experience satisfaction at the same time they suffer the pain, despair, and limitations that come from having experienced trauma. In fact, in their review of the literature on resilient children, Masten and Coatsworth (1998) question whether being resilient may actually increase psychological distress.

Resilient adults often struggle against despair and continued pain. Steven and Sybil Wolin, a psychiatrist and psychologist who are a husband and wife team, wrote a useful book, *The Resilient Self:*

How Survivors of Troubled Families Rise Above Adversity (1993).
They conclude that for most people "resilience and vulnerability
are in steady opposition. . . . The inner life of the typical survivor is
a battleground where the forces of discouragement and the forces
of determination constantly clash. For many determination wins
out" (p. 6).

Psychiatrist Frederic Flach goes further. He argues that even life
disruption is not necessarily incompatible with resilience. "Falling
apart" does not necessarily mean someone is not resilient but can
at times be a necessary first step in personal renewal. According to
Flach (1988), resilience is "the psychological and biological strengths
required to successfully master change" (p. xi). Many resilient individuals recognize they need help, seek it, find new ways of dealing
with life, and consider the disruption in life to be an opportunity.
We saw, and other researchers have noted, that resiliency does not
mean that survivors have moved beyond pain, although getting to a
place with less pain and more joy was important and was occurring
in their lives.

A TRANSACTIONAL FRAMEWORK

The transactional model specifies that through interaction over
time, the child and her environment will evolve and change each
other. Just as parents influence their children, for example, children
also influence their parents. A classroom has an impact on a child,
and that child influences the classroom, in particular how the
teacher and the other children respond to him or her. Several implications stem from the use of this transactional model. First, a
person's ability to cope with adversity or trauma depends on the
availability of personal resources and social support at the time of
the difficult events. Second, even with good enough support, an
individual must be able to make use of her personal strengths and
the social supports available to successfully resolve her difficulties.
Finally, an individual acts on her environment even as it acts on

her, and over time the changes that occur are both transactional and developmental. Being successful in dealing with her environment is likely to make the individual more resilient.

Most researchers who take the transactional framework emphasize that resilience is not a fixed quality or set of characteristics; rather, it operates through numerous processes and in interaction with the environment, which includes biological, psychological, and environmental factors. Taking the developmental and transactional frameworks seriously makes the scientific study of resilience exceedingly complex and difficult.

We found this framework particularly helpful in understanding such complex interactional stories as the ways changes in our participants and the ways consequent interactions with relatives caused changes in the family dynamics; those family changes in turn allowed the survivors to relate in different ways and to learn something more about themselves.

THE CHAPTERS THAT FOLLOW

This book was written to tell therapists about resilience, to suggest ways to think about it, and to encourage them to see aspects of it even in the most vulnerable and struggling clients. We believe conceptualizing it in the ways we have, and learning to notice and nurture it, can offer powerful tools to clinicians working with survivors, whether in very brief therapies or work lasting many years. Learning about resilience has opened our eyes to the impressive capacity to go through horrible life experiences and emerge, although scarred, able to love and to work, and at times to have a depth, richness, compassion, and courage that would not otherwise have been possible.

In the remaining chapters, we apply our perspective on resiliency first to the various contexts of survivors' lives—their settings and relationships. We then turn our focus to crucial resilient processes: the management of feelings, self-care, and meaning making.

We end the book with what we learned in the follow-up interviews five to eight years after the initial contacts. These interviews delighted us by confirming our view of these women as resilient, despite the serious problems some still struggled with, and by reinforcing our view of what processes were important in their continuing recovery. The follow-up interviews also supported us in our hopeful belief that survivors of serious childhood sexual abuse can heal, with the help of good psychotherapy, and in that process of recovery can develop a richness, humanity, and depth that many people with more fortunate histories never achieve.

2

The Women's Stories

At the beginning of this study, we struggled with how best to learn about resiliency. So much research is based on questionnaires and statistical analyses that, in the end, much is learned about numbers and little about people's lives. We wanted to give voice to survivors, who have too often been silenced and who have important knowledge to impart to those of us in mental health professions. For these and other reasons, we decided to learn through interviews. (Details of our method can be found in the Appendix and in Grossman, Kruger, & Moore, 1999.)

In our search for resilient women survivors, we posted notices in clinics, academic centers, and women's bookstores; we also sent descriptions of the study to colleagues who are therapists. The women who responded found us in different ways. Sisters, friends, psychotherapists, and other participants referred some; others responded to fliers. We heard from many women and finally selected ten who we felt represented as wide a range of ages, backgrounds, races, and sexual orientations as we could find. Using a variety of measures, we interviewed each for five to ten hours at the beginning of the project. (We interviewed them again briefly, after they had read the nearly complete manuscript, five to eight years later. The results of those last interviews are described in Chapter Eleven.) The interviews

---

Note: Katherine Culhane was a coauthor of this chapter.

were taped, transcribed, and analyzed using a qualitative research method, with the resulting stories filtered through our many years of accumulated clinical experience. The direct quotes were altered only to the extent necessary to make them easier to read. In this chapter, we offer a sense of who each of our participants is, as we came to know her in the initial interviews. The best place to start is with their own words.

ANNE

> The whole idea of when life gives you lemons, make lemonade. So yeah, I guess phrasing it in the positive sometimes comes across as being a little pollyanna, but with all the layers of pain underneath it all, if anybody thinks it's pollyanna they've missed the point, because there's so many layers of pain.

Anne has worked very hard and quite successfully throughout her life to make lemonade from lemons. The lemons were not immediately obvious when we first met her, at age forty-five. She was married, a mother of four apparently thriving adolescents, with whom she described close relationships; she was an active member of her church community and a music teacher. She had friends and relationships with an extended family.

As we got to know her better in over ten hours of interviewing, she told us about some of the rough edges in her current life. Her marriage was perhaps the most painful to her. She was increasingly unhappy in her relationship with her husband of twenty-five years but did not see a way, economically or psychologically, to leave. She was struggling with some physical problems and with her relationship with one of her two sisters.

She told us the story of her childhood, as she was beginning to understand it through her individual and couple's therapy, particularly after the death of her parents six years earlier. Anne was the middle child (with two sisters) of an upper-middle-class, north-western family. She told us that she could trace her family back to the American Revolution and described with pride several generations of successful and achieving women. Her mother was cultured and committed to using her abilities and energy in creative volunteer activities, and to passing this cultural heritage on to her children. Her father, an upper-middle-class professional, was highly regarded in their community, winning honors such as being elected Man of the Year.

However, the family had its "weirdness," to use Anne's word. Her mother's problematic boundaries ranged from bizarre and inappropriate behavior such as appearing naked in the dining room wearing only buttons on her nipples to repeatedly giving all three daughters enemas in a ritualistic and sadistic manner. Shortly before coming to our first interview, Anne had received a letter from her older sister stating that the sister had been sexually abused repeatedly by their father, with assistance from their mother. The information threw into doubt her extremely positive view of her father and made her wonder whether he had abused her as well.

Although during her first year of college Anne saw a psychiatrist to deal with suicidal feelings, she finished college, married her teenage sweetheart, and had four children; later she began to focus on her career in music. She and her husband had begun couple's therapy fifteen years before our interview. When he refused to return to couple's therapy, Anne continued individual therapy for six years.

Anne credited her humor, which she had learned in her family of origin, as an important source of her resiliency. Further, she was committed to maintaining a positive approach to life. She had begun to write and publish poetry—an important avenue for expression of her feelings and the hard-won wisdom she had gained. Although she probably has strengths that she would not have developed without going through the crucible of childhood trauma, she has paid dearly for those strengths.

ILONA

I start thinking just a little bit of the enormity! The enormity of everything, of all the negativity in my formative years, my very fragile and my formative years, and that's when I started to think, Wow! Look what you've overcome! I have tossed out the word *miracle* rather loosely, but I have to realize that these things did happen to me . . . and they happened to other women. . . . And how do you get beyond it? . . . My survival skills were such that I was able to get above and beyond all this garbage that was going on in my life. But now at this stage, at sixty years old, it's about time I said to myself, "Look what you've done with your life, despite all this stuff!"

We agree about the enormity of the abuse and neglect in Ilona's childhood and, like Ilona, were impressed and amazed at how well she had survived it all. When we interviewed her, Ilona at sixty was a mother and in a second marriage that had lasted many years. Her husband, who died shortly after the interviews, was a personnel manager. She had two grown children with whom she had complicated relationships. Several years prior to our interviews Ilona had completed her high school requirements and then received an undergraduate degree. She retired from a clerical job and at the time of the interviews was studying for a master's degree in human services and was working with learning-disabled children. She loved both her academic and her current work experiences.

Ilona's parents had been immigrant Russian Jews. When she was five, her parents divorced; her brother and her father went to live in another city. Ilona lived with her mother, who worked as a waitress in a gambling house and later as a switchboard operator. When she was young, Ilona and her mother lived in a small neighborhood hotel, Ilona always in a separate room. On her own for meals, she generally looked out for herself. The only person she remembered being close to in childhood was Brenda, a woman old enough to be her grandmother, who lived at the hotel and befriended her. Between her eleventh and fourteenth years, Ilona sometimes ate with her. When she was fourteen, she stopped going to school. Periodically, her mother would send her away to live with various strangers, or occasionally relatives, in different cities.

Ilona has an extensive history of physical and sexual abuse and neglect. The most salient are the emotional abuse and neglect by her mother. She suffered the first sexual abuse when she was five, by a man in one of the gambling houses where her mother worked. When she was nine or ten, one of her mother's lovers sexually abused her. Neighborhood boys forced her to masturbate them. She was date raped at sixteen.

About sixteen years before the interviews, she had begun to attend Overeaters Anonymous to deal with her obesity. As she gained more awareness of her relationship to food, she saw she had been "stuffing" her feelings down. She stopped doing that and gradually began to more fully remember and then to deal with her exceedingly neglectful and abusive history. Beginning in her late fifties, after she had obtained her high school equivalency diploma and attended college, she began therapy. We see Ilona as a sturdy survivor of an awful history and as an example for others of courage and persistence in living life.

BETH

One of the things that really helped me was I'm really smart, and I learned how to use my intelligence to get by in the world. I mean I'm also a terribly rational person, and I think there's a real advantage in this society for being rational—we reward people who are terribly rational, and I think I'm lucky because my reaction to these things was to get depressed and become an overachiever.

I didn't go into prostitution, I didn't become an alcoholic, I didn't get into drugs, so I'd go off and get straight A's, and read all the books. . . . So I think that's what really got me through it.

Beth's intelligence, rationality, and ability to work hard to achieve have been major factors in her resiliency. When we met her, she was thirty-seven, had an M.B.A., and was earning more than $60,000 at a high-level job in a prestigious academic institution. Although she did not really like her job because it did not speak to her heart, she understood that it allowed her to pursue her recovery by making affordable all the kinds of psychotherapy she was in during the intense phase of her healing. And she was able to take tuition-free courses to explore her new interest—writing. She stated that she had many good friends and an active social life.

Her ten-year-old son lived with his father in the Midwest as a result of an ugly custody fight, but Beth talked to him often and saw him monthly. They seemed to have a good relationship.

Beth was the third of five children of divorced parents, with three sisters and one brother. Her father had been a physician; her mother was a homemaker and part-time nurse for her husband. Beth was reared in an upper-middle-class life in the Midwest. There was a strong family history of depression and alcoholism. Beth's mother had been hospitalized for depression when Beth was in the fourth grade; to Beth, she appeared to be very troubled. In addition, at the time of the initial interviews, she said that one of her older sisters had also been hospitalized for depression several times.

At the time we first talked with her, Beth was in the process of recovering memories of multiple kinds of abuse. What she knew then was that she had been molested repeatedly and forcefully by an eleven-year-old neighborhood boy when she was four. When she was a young adolescent and beginning to menstruate, her mother twice forcibly tried to insert a tampon into her vagina. She was given a gynecological exam by her father, a physician, when she was a young adult. In the follow-up interviews, she told us she had remembered being raped by an uncle over a period of years.

Beth decided to move away from her home and attend a prestigious college despite family pressure to remain close to home. After college, she married a man she did not know well who was leaving immediately to work in Europe. That was a very hard time for her, as she was extremely isolated and was gradually learning how emotionally abusive her husband was. After she got pregnant, it became clear to her that she did not need to remain in the life she was leading. She and her husband relocated to an American community in Paris, at Beth's insistence, and she began to reclaim her selfhood. When she returned to this country, Beth began divorce proceedings. There was a terrible custody fight, and her husband was given physical custody of their five-year-old son, of whom Beth had been the primary caretaker. During the last months of her marriage, she became very depressed and sought help when she lost a great deal of weight and essentially stopped talking, eating, and sleeping. In the interview Beth said that during the process of grieving the loss of her son, with the help of a psychotherapist, she developed the strength to begin to confront, remember, and ultimately grieve her history of abuse. She had been in multiple modalities of treatment since then, including group and individual therapy, and hypnosis for memory retrieval.

Her strengths and resiliency were very evident when we saw her. She was planning for a shift to a career that promised much more satisfaction. She had started a support group for mothers without custody and was planning to write a book about that experience. She had developed a strong support network, including a church community with a sympathetic assistant pastor. Unlike some of our participants, Beth did see some of what she had gained from her difficult life experiences but also reminded us of the daily pain her abusive history still brought her.

DARLENE

I have no understanding of why it happened. Kids who abuse you have to have gotten it from some place, so it's most likely that they were abused or had something awful happen to them. And I feel that may have been the case and that may not have been the case, I don't really know. . . . I don't think I'll ever know, and I've just reached a point where knowing why is not the important thing in me coming to terms with everything that happened, and my ability to keep going in life.

At the time of the initial interviews, Darlene was very clear about her priorities of "keeping going in her life," completing her doctoral training in psychology, working in therapy, and looking forward rather than backward. She was thirty years old and had recently separated from her lesbian partner after a six-year relationship. She had several close friends and two important mentors, one an African American woman who was also her dissertation adviser.

Darlene was the only girl, with older and younger brothers, and grew up in a working-class African American family with many, close extended-family ties in a large southwestern city. Darlene's parents divorced when she was two, but her father spent time with her and her siblings. He was a factory worker with some college education. Her mother had attended high school and had a clerical job. Both at home and at school, Darlene was recognized as being very smart at a very young age.

Although most of her mother's relatives were alcoholics, the three siblings were drug-free and her parents did not drink. Unlike her brothers, Darlene was not beaten by either of her parents, which she attributed to the fact that she was smart and well behaved.

Darlene was physically abused by her older brother. She told us that at the time she had appealed to her mother for help but was refused. She was also repeatedly and violently abused, both physically and sexually, from age three to thirteen by two much older female cousins who frequently babysat her and other younger cousins. She was first raped at age eight. At around ten, her cousins' boyfriends also began to abuse her and her cousins' younger siblings. Darlene was also forced to perform sexual acts on her younger cousins.

Darlene described herself as accident-prone in childhood and self-abusive in adolescence. She tried to kill herself when she was fourteen, and her father took her to a hospital; no one offered her psychiatric treatment then. When Darlene was sixteen, she suffered the death of her much-beloved maternal grandmother, with whom she had her closest relationship and who was a haven of safety. She went through a terrible depression in which she did not speak for many months. It was then that she began her first counseling relationship, with a high school counselor.

Darlene always remembered the abuse. During college, she began therapy to deal with it. In 1986, five years before our interview with her, Darlene confronted her mother about what had happened. Her mother was receptive and concerned. Darlene became increasingly depressed and suicidal and then was convinced by her therapist to accept a voluntary hospitalization. Darlene was very angry during several months of hospitalization and through the next year of therapy. It was a difficult time, but then she settled into what seemed to be a productive and cooperative period in therapy. A year before we interviewed her, riding the elevator to her therapist's office, she was digitally raped by a white man.

Despite the difficulties and setbacks, Darlene was determined that nothing was going to interfere with moving ahead in her career and her life; she showed enormous resilience in those endeavors. She knew, as we did, that being an African American woman had complicated her history as well as her therapy. Further, we were aware that it complicated her participation in the research project. She expressed some of that complexity:

Sometimes I feel very different when I'm with white women and they're sharing their experiences. . . . In dealing with the abuse, I know one thing, and that was really prominent in my family, no matter what the issue was, what goes on in this house stays in this house. And I think that was even more rigid when it came to dealing with white people and white systems as far as letting them into your community and into your home and into your family. And so in a sense when I talk about stuff I still feel like I'm telling and I'm breaking a sort of boundary and a family code. . . . Just growing up, one of the things that was always said a lot was how protective we were, you know, blacks to one another, and how we have to stick together. And it feels like much more some kind of violation that black people did this to me. And so it's really difficult to come to terms with.

At one point, she talked about learning from her experiences that "you can be horribly abused and still survive that and go on and make a life for yourself. I think that's hard and that can sometimes involve a lot of struggle. But with every accomplishment I feel more like, 'Yes, I definitely can do that.'"

CARRIE

I think you have to, every little bit of health that you've got, every little bit of love that you've gotten in your whole life, I think you have to draw on to deal with, to try to comfort yourself or heal.

Carrie is an example of a survivor who, despite serious incestuous abuse, had gotten some love in her life. Carrie had some close and nurturing ties within her family, especially with her mother.

That connection allowed her to feel loved at times and to have more trust in relationships than the other study participants.

At the time of the initial interviews, Carrie was twenty-nine, single, and living in a Boston suburb with two roommates. She had been in a happy, stable, intimate relationship with a man for eight months. Judaism and feminism were sources of strength for her. She loved her job as a manager in a halfway house for mentally ill adults and was planning to complete her master's in psychology. She realized that taking care of others was a way of caring for herself, and her work helped her make meaning of her experiences.

Her grandparents on both sides were first- and second-generation Polish-Russian-Jewish immigrants. Carrie's father was a prominent businessman and her mother an administrative assistant; they lived in the southeastern part of the country. By all appearances, it was a close family when Carrie was born. When she was two, her sister was born. While her mother was in the hospital, Carrie's father sexually abused her. The abuse continued until she was five years old and then occurred again at a difficult point in her father's life when Carrie was nine. She described her father as distant and controlling, and prone to wild rages. Up until then, Carrie had a very close relationship with her mother, but after the birth of another child, a distance developed that has continued. She told us she always felt older than her mother and felt she needed to parent her rather than the other way around.

She went to a women's college and began weekly therapy during her second year there. At the end of that year she knew something was wrong, although she had no memory of abuse. She decided to leave college in an attempt to heal. A year later she went back and finished school. She worked for four years after college and then, at twenty-six, began a graduate program. At that point she joined a young adult therapy group. It was a discussion of group members' relationships with their fathers that precipitated her first memories of the incest. At that point, she sought individual therapy to work on the abuse.

Carrie had always had close relationships with a number of people, including members of her extended family, friends, and mentors. For many years, however, she had little relationship with her father. Shortly before the interviews, she had confronted her parents with the abuse. According to Carrie, her mother had not known how to respond, and things were strained between them. Despite her anger and pain, Carrie was very protective of her father's identity, not wanting to jeopardize his considerable status.

Although Carrie understood that she had gained a capacity to empathize with people in pain that she might not have had without the abuse, she thought she would have been sensitive without those traumatic experiences. She concluded: "This is a part of who I am and somehow in creating meaningful work or in making meaning in my life I'm going to have to turn this around. . . . If something bad happens to you, you've got to use it to make something good." She was working hard and effectively to do just that.

ELENA

When I turned thirty-eight, that was when I felt like I'd gotten my life back. . . . Out of that pain and out of things, I've gained a me that I never had.

It was crucial to Elena to regain the "me," and she was working very hard to do so. When we first interviewed her, she was thirty-nine and held a high-status job as director of a prestigious master's degree program. Although she felt she was working too hard in her present position, she enjoyed the pay, content, power, and prestige. She had earned both an M.S. in engineering and an M.B.A. At the time of the interview, Elena had a lesbian lover with whom she jointly owned a home. She said the two of them hoped to have children.

Elena grew up in an upper-middle-class Jewish family in an affluent area of New York. She had an older brother; her father was a dentist; her mother worked in the home and as a volunteer in the

Jewish community. Elena described her family and her childhood as isolated, with an emphasis on order. She recalled her father having a bad temper; no one else in the family was allowed to get angry. Elena said that her most important relationship was with her mother. Her mother was the only person with whom she felt connected as a child.

For most of her life, Elena told us, she remembered very little about her childhood. At the time of the interviews, she thought she first began to remember the abuse after participating in an EST (Ehrhardt Sensitivity Training) workshop. (These workshops, popular in the 1970s, were large-group, weekend-long therapeutic meetings that some in the field believed resembled cults.) What she felt confident about knowing at the time of the initial interviews was that she had been abused by her father for years. The abuse progressed from his making her sit on his lap and then fondling her, to coming to her bed at night, to finally taking her to his office and making her sit in the dental chair, then fondling her breasts and genitals and penetrating her with his fingers. The abuse ended sometime between her eleventh and fourteenth years.

Elena also said she had been molested by three or four adults when she was in a nursery school, and she thought she had been abused by her maternal grandfather, who died when she was three.

Her brother told Elena, who did not remember it, that their parents quarreled constantly and their father would scream at their mother. She did recall fearing her father's verbal abuse. Her mother tried to protect her children from his anger. Elena was not aware of any other physical abuse.

None of the abuse Elena experienced as a child was ever talked about. It remained a large and destructive secret in a fairly intact and organized family. But Elena confronted her father as an adult and told her mother. Her father apologized, and there had been a gradual resumption of some contact between herself and her father.

For the previous fifteen years, Elena had been on a quest to heal. The pursuit of this quest led her to a variety of settings, among them many years of individual psychotherapy, as well as EST workshops, Model Mugging (self-defense training with a particular appeal for abuse survivors), psychodrama, a workshop with Ellen Bass, author of *The Courage to Heal* (Bass & Davis, 1988), and a high-ropes course. At times the energy she directed toward healing was almost consuming. She said, "When I've been . . . healing, actively healing, then I can barely find the energy to talk to anybody or want to." When we interviewed her at age thirty-nine, she said she felt as though she had finally begun to move from surviving to living.

In addition to her relationship with her partner and her engagement in psychotherapy and related activities, Elena pointed to her faith as providing an avenue toward healing. She described to us a night when she was feeling particularly lonely and afraid and "brought God into the healing." She asked God to help her not be afraid and promised in return to attend services at a synagogue. After that, she and her partner became members of a synagogue and began to attend services frequently.

She was feeling very good about herself and her life at the time of the initial interviews, and even more so at the follow-up. She felt blessed and confident that her life would keep getting better and better.

FELICIA

As a kid I was very wise and very much more advanced . . . . I would pretty much isolate myself from [other kids], and I used to like to read a lot. So basically I knew bad things happen to people, but you had to go on. I would just take things as they came. And try to use common sense about things. I remember when I was little, I read on someone's desk, "This moment, it'll pass. It's not going to be like this all the time." And I remembered that.

Felicia was thirty-six years old and living in Boston when we first talked with her. She had an associate degree and was on leave from a local university where she had been working on her bachelor's degree. Felicia had been receiving disability payments since her third hospitalization two years before. At the beginning of our interviews with her, she was working an average of forty hours a week as a volunteer and getting a great deal of satisfaction from it. Some of her volunteer activities were based on skills and knowledge she had developed in her previous jobs as a security guard. An African American woman, she contributed an enormous amount to her community, including volunteering at a community health center and for a community development corporation, sitting on a neighborhood advisory board for the local police department, and contributing to neighborhood safety programs. In the recent past, Felicia had begun a lesbian dialogue group, founded a lesbian-bisexual group, and participated in a lesbian-gay speakers' bureau. After our second interview, she was recruited for and took a part-time, salaried job with a community newspaper.

Felicia had a committed lesbian partner. They maintained separate apartments and shared a cat. She said she had no close friends, although she thought some people probably considered her their close friend.

She grew up as the much younger of two daughters in an inner-city family. Her grandparents on both sides had been alcoholic. Her father was emotionally abusive to her mother, who retaliated with physical violence. At some point during Felicia's childhood, her father left the household and moved to another city. Felicia told us that her mother physically abused both children. She described herself as a loner, a sad child; she saw her birth as an accident and her life as fragmented. She said she had felt close only to her paternal grandmother, who considered her special. From the interviews, we felt there had also been a significant attachment between herself and her sister, older by seven years, who had tried in some ways to look out for her.

Felicia was not much involved in institutional religions, but her spiritual life was very important to her and a great source of strength. She read widely and had done so since she was very young. She was able to use information from her reading to make sense of her life and in some ways comfort herself.

Both the son and nephew of Felicia's babysitter began sexually abusing her when she was about four or five, often several times a week. She told her mother about the abuse, but her mother did not believe her. At the time of the interviews, she believed that her father had some idea of what was going on, because when she was nine or ten, her father came and took her out of school and to a different part of the country where his sister lived. Felicia lived with this aunt for two years, and she described that period as her happiest. On false pretenses, promising it was just for a visit, her mother got her back and kept her. Shortly thereafter, Felicia made a serious suicide attempt.

When she was seventeen, her father offered to take her away again. He helped her pack up, took her to another city, gave her $1,000 to get started, and left her there alone. Eventually she got a job working as a security guard and started to do very well in her employment. She quickly was given more responsibility. As part of her job in security, she was dealing with a situation of alleged abuse at the workplace. This was extremely stressful for her. She developed what was later diagnosed as a conversion disorder, with major paralysis of her legs and other parts of her body. During her first hospitalization, she was also diagnosed with PTSD and bipolar disorder. Over a relatively brief period of time, she had two more hospitalizations before it became clear to her that she needed to follow the doctors' orders and do some serious work in psychotherapy.

Felicia always knew that she had been sexually abused and was clear about those events. She also knew that she had dissociated during some of those events. She had no money to pay for therapy so had received state-funded care, one consequence being that her therapists were mostly trainees and tended to rotate out of the hospital or clinic. Despite this, Felicia had forged strong relationships with several of her therapists and had done considerable work. At the time of the interviews, she was in psychotherapy twice weekly and saw her psychopharmacologist every other week.

When she summed up for us what she thought she had gained from the experience, she talked about becoming more compassionate and committed to treating people by the Golden Rule.

GALEN

> Being working class or poor is something that is very invisible in America because of classism and because of the way that this society's set up. Especially if you're white. . . . It's hard because I'm often assumed to be middle class. At college, my friends would come from very different backgrounds like in terms of being middle class or upper middle class. It feels like a very cultural difference to me. . . . It's a different language, it's different ways of viewing the world, it's different social ideas, like a different culture in a way.

It was very important to Galen that we understand the working-class world that she came from and how that colored the abuse she experienced, as well as the process she had gone through to heal from it. When we interviewed Galen at age twenty-six, she was working with a local program for formerly homeless adults with diagnoses of mental illness. She was not earning much money and was in disagreement with the program's traditional approach to mental health, having worked previously in a feminist, relational environment. She had finished college and was currently living with a lesbian lover whom she had gotten to know in college. She felt her relative impoverishment strongly and resented the difficulties it placed in her path toward getting further schooling and developing her career.

Galen grew up as the only girl, with an older and a younger brother in a poor, working-class midwestern community. She described her former home as a violent place where her father tyrannized the family and the children abused one another in a chain reaction. Her mother, the daughter of Czechoslovakian immigrants, was battered by her husband and was unable to defend her children. She described three generations of alcoholism and sexual and physical abuse in the family.

Galen was sexually and physically abused by her father from the time she was between two and four years old until she was around fourteen. She wanted us to understand that his sexual abuse was not the behind-closed-doors sort that involved intercourse but rather a constant violation of emotional and physical boundaries that had strong sexual components. She remembered feeling alone, trapped, separate from her mother, and inseparable from her father. She understood at the time of the interviews that she had dissociated when her father was violent and abusive and referred to having lost blocks of time and parts of her childhood. An uncle was sexually involved with her in much the same way her father had been, from the time she was a young teen until her early twenties. She told us that school helped her survive those years, as she could escape into her mind's "own perfect world."

Galen had not always remembered all of the abuse in her history and had not always interpreted the boundary violations as abuse. She began drinking and smoking cigarettes and marijuana when she was thirteen and continued to do so through most of her college days. In the interview, she described herself as having been promiscuous with women in the past. She had come out as a lesbian in the two years out of school between her freshman and sophomore years in college. When she was twenty-two, she worked in a shelter for battered women as part of her college work requirement and then went on to work in a halfway house for women who were mostly abuse survivors. Around that time, she made the decision to become sober; she stopped using alcohol and marijuana. Shortly afterward, she started having memories of her own abuse. At that point, she sought help from a therapist. At the time of our interviews, she had been sober for four years.

A major source of Galen's resiliency was the philosophical perspective provided by her understanding of how issues of classism and sexism had influenced her life. In some ways, she had suffered as much from working-class homophobia as from the sexual abuse itself. Her clarity about these issues provided a handle and framework for dealing with her experiences and feelings, and we feel she is dealing very well and will continue to grow.

HELEN

> I still get that not-to-speak stuff, like when I hear them talking about false memory syndrome. And it's just like, maybe they're right, but I know there are other people out there like me. Who cares about publicity or anything like that? There's someone else out there that feels the way I do, and if they need the help, they can talk to me about it.

Helen had developed the conviction that she needed to speak about her experiences of incest and satanic cult abuse, even though she clearly understood that many people did not want to hear about such things. At the time of the interviews, Helen was a single, twenty-nine-year-old woman, employed as a bookkeeper and living with a roommate; she had a high school education and hoped to go to college. Helen had recently resumed participation in the Catholic religion. She wanted to have relationships and closeness but found it hard to do so, especially with women. She wasn't in an intimate relationship when we interviewed her and, at the time, described having two close friends.

Helen was the oldest child in her family of origin, with four full or half brothers and sisters. Her parents divorced when she was ten;

before and after the divorce, Helen felt responsible for the care of her siblings. Her father was a prosperous grocery store owner. Her mother, a homemaker who had part-time jobs and sometimes prostituted herself, died a homeless alcoholic five years before our interviews. After her parents separated, Helen lived with her mother, her mother's boyfriend, and her siblings. She described their socioeconomic status as changing then from middle class to lower class. Six years later, she and her siblings forced their mother to leave their home because she was an alcoholic and drug addict, and their father returned to live there. Helen did not see her mother for three years. The family's financial situation improved. She knew that her mother was an abuse survivor. Although she wondered if her mother had multiple personalities, she was certain she was mentally ill. She believed that at least one sibling had multiple personality disorder. Although she did not apply that label to herself at the time of the initial interviews, she was wondering if she was suffering from that disorder as well. By the follow-up interview she had been told by a psychiatrist that she did not have dissociative identity disorder (multiple personality). Helen told us about three generations of substance abuse, including abuse of cocaine, marijuana, and alcohol.

Helen described herself as someone who dissociated, as an alcoholic, and as an incest and satanic cult abuse survivor; she was used by the cult from birth until age twenty-four. (We were acutely aware that this was not many years before we first met her, and at the time of the initial interviews we had some concerns about her physical and emotional safety.) Although she had always remembered the emotional abuse by her mother, she had been less clear about the sexual abuse by her father and the satanic ritual abuse, which she began remembering two years before the interviews. She had been told that her mother's boyfriend beat her but did not remember that. She told us that her father's family was actively involved in the satanic cult and that she had been used as a breeder for the cult. She did not know how often she had been pregnant, but she did tell us that her last pregnancy was when she was twenty-four or twenty-five. As far as she knew, she had no living children.

She began abusing alcohol at age thirteen, and marijuana and cocaine before that. She had been sober for three and one-half years at the time of the initial interviews and was in recovery from anorexia and bulimia. During the year or so before the interviews, she was hospitalized twice, for a month each time. When we interviewed her she was in a twelve-step program, as well as group and individual psychotherapy.

When asked what she had gained or learned from her abusive experiences, she responded: "Knowledge. It's like weapons, it's a tool. . . . I've learned more about the mind. As far as lessons, or what's the moral of the story, I have no idea what it is. I just do have faith that whatever it is [is] going to come out later, just follow the light."

JANET

I think I always had an inner strength, and I always had faith, and I've always felt a spiritual presence in my life. So I always felt like I could survive. I always felt in spite of it all some kind of overall protection.

Janet was surviving—and more—when we interviewed her. At that time she was forty-two, a social worker with a private practice of psychotherapy. She was only moderately satisfied with her work. She was living with her husband, a Jewish man with whom she described having a good relationship, and their two young children. They were not affiliated with any religion. She told us about several close friendships with people who she felt were very supportive of her and her healing.

Janet was the second-oldest of five children from a lower-middle-class, Irish-Catholic family who lived in a small northeastern town. There were at least four generations of alcoholics that she could identify, including her father. Both parents had violent backgrounds, which likely included sexual as well as physical abuse. Janet described family life as chaotic. She left home the day she graduated from high school, lived briefly with an aunt, then went away first to college and then to get her master's degree in social work. At the time of the interviews, Janet had a close relationship with one sister and had maintained some distant contact with her parents and most of her other siblings.

Janet told us she had been singled out for material deprivation as a child and later. She never had adequate clothes and never was allowed to go to events that cost any money. She paid her own college tuition, although her parents financed a sister's tuition at an expensive private college. Later her father tried to make up for that by treating his children more equally.

In a therapy session the day before our first interview, Janet had confronted her parents with her abuse history. Between the ages of six and twelve she had been physically abused by her parents about every other week. Her older brother was sadistic and abused his siblings emotionally and physically. An aunt and uncle with whom she stayed some summers also abused her physically and her uncle abused her sexually. Her father sexually abused her when she was very young, under six. Her mother observed an incident of incest when Janet was six, and after that singled her out for ridicule, deprivation, and beatings.

Janet said that she had been promiscuous and abused drugs when she was in college and afterward. When she was twenty-three, she was raped and sexually abused by a man she was involved with. At about age twenty-five, Janet worked as a poker dealer in Las Vegas. She acknowledged that she took many unnecessary risks and that there were other incidents of sexual abuse at that time in her life. She had been suicidal in college and in her twenties and early thirties.

Janet had participated in group therapy for survivors of sexual abuse and was working with a trauma therapist when we interviewed her. She had just taken very strong stands with her family of origin, setting limits on her contacts with them and insisting on appropriate behavior from them. It was hard for her to do, but she was determined and seemed to be doing it successfully.

When asked what she had gained or learned from her experience, Janet said simply, "I have learned to be a healer and to really empathize with other people's pain." Later in the interview she said, regarding her own learning, "I'm stronger in my own truth now. I know that this is my truth and it doesn't matter if there's denial around it or if other people in the family don't see it that way."

WHERE WE GO FROM HERE

These then are the participants whose stories have taught us so much about resiliency. These brief summaries illustrate why they or their therapist considered them resilient. They all had notable strengths in the face of painful and difficult childhood histories of abuse. We also saw their vulnerabilities, more in some than in others. We believed they had a lot to teach us about resiliency, whether or not in the long run their strengths or their weaknesses prevailed. (We were delighted to discover in the follow-up interviews that their resiliency did prevail, in very impressive and striking ways, but we did not know that when we drafted all but the last chapter of this book.)

In the next section, we focus on the contexts of these women's lives—their work and school settings and their various important relationships. Throughout, we emphasize their resiliency—ways they were able to prevail over their histories—and not the ways they were less successful in doing that. We believe both sides are crucial in understanding the lives of survivors, but the weaknesses and psychopathology have been described in many books and articles. Our focus here is on the ways things can go right.

Part II

Safe Havens, Important Relationships

3

School and Work

In this chapter we focus on our participants' resiliency in the context of their school and work lives. We found their resilience in these settings particularly remarkable because it was clear that, for many of them, no matter what was happening in other aspects of their lives or relationships, school and work were areas in which they continued to do well and to gain a positive sense of themselves. This was true for all participants, even though they varied in educational attainment, income, and satisfaction in their work. Participants' ability to find safety, self-esteem, and opportunities for growth in relationships through school and work reflected their resiliency and gave them a foundation of greater strength and stability from which to pursue further growth and healing.

SCHOOL

Our participants had a variety of experiences with school that supported their ever-growing resiliency. In the sections to follow we discuss the topics that were most salient in their stories. First we point out that, for many of these women, one benefit they received from their often-abusive families was support for, and emphasis on, academic excellence. Next we show how school relationships sometimes provided a healing antidote to abusive and neglectful home relationships. Then we describe how school success had different meanings in the lives of these women. For some it provided a source of self-esteem and a chance to escape the abuse at home. In the last section we show that the choices our participants made about schooling significantly contributed to their later opportunities for growth and healing. We were particularly struck by that. Turning points in their recovery often revolved around going away to school, which provided the separation from family that was necessary for the women to make significant strides toward healing.

Family Support for Academic Excellence

No matter how abusive parents are, they are rarely all bad, and the abusive parents of resilient survivors frequently have significant strengths; they often give important positive aspects of parenting to their children. This contradiction often complicates an adult child's feelings toward her abusive family. The benefits an adult child received and continues to receive from her family, in terms of encouragement or financial support, serve to maintain her bond with that family. In the case of our participants, we often found that abusive parents were to varying degrees still able to encourage their child's success in the outside world; over half cited their parents' emphasis on education as a driving force behind their success in school.

Carrie, who was seriously abused by her father, cited wanting to please her father as a major force behind her drive to excel in school. She told us: "It was very important for me to aspire to college, very important for me to go to college, and actually I was supposed to do great things. Basically, I was supposed to follow his footsteps." Although she was ambivalent about this desire to please her father, her success in school was ultimately adaptive and had important implications for her future success. For a number of our participants, school success enabled them to become financially independent and support themselves well, which in turn had positive effects on their lives.

Galen was one of the few participants who came from a working-class background. Neither of her parents had been to college, but they encouraged her to pursue an education. Galen said, "My mom was pretty excited about my achievements and . . . she wanted me to go beyond what she was able to do with her life." Similarly, she told us, her father "always wanted me to be like a lawyer or a doctor, which is kind of funny. I read somewhere too, fathers who abuse their daughters, a lot of times they want them to be like what they couldn't be; they identify with them. I was the one who got really good grades, so my Dad thought I should go to college, and so he would always say that to me."

So parental support for academic achievement was an important factor in our participants' resiliency. Masten and Coatsworth (1998) point out, following their review of the resiliency literature, that a number of other researchers have found the same thing.

That these women could take their families' encouragement and excel in school while being abused at home is certainly a reflection of their resilience; they were performing well at school at the very time they were being terrorized and hurt at home. Success in school provided them with further resilience, at least in part because it helped them leave home and begin the long road to recovery. That the parents could provide this support reflects their strengths without denying the vulnerability and pathology that led them to abuse their children.

In addition to the benefits the participants gained from such family support for school achievement, we saw that finding strength from their family histories helped them see their families in a broader and more accurate perspective, both the terrible weaknesses and the helpful, life-giving characteristics. Perceiving this about their families also helped these women see themselves more fully and accurately. At the follow-up interview Galen told us that she had come to see her father differently and no longer viewed him as simply evil. She told us, "To see him as more complex has helped me to see myself as more complex." Seeing the positive aspects of their families also reduced the sense of shame many had about their families and helped some to feel compassion for their parents and become reconciled with one or more family members.

We encourage psychotherapists to listen carefully for clients' stories about the positive things they took from their families and to wonder, along with the clients, about these stories. This will let survivors make family strengths a conscious part of their narrative when they are ready. We also caution therapists against setting the pace. At different points in recovery, the survivor may need to see all good or all bad in her family before she can hold both. She is the expert on when the time is right.

Clinicians can support clients' resilience by acknowledging the good that, however distorted by abuse, was available in their families. Although many clients need to expand the awareness of their anger, most struggle with feelings of ambivalence. Having this ambivalence validated and normalized supports each woman's ability to hold complex and contradictory feelings simultaneously. Therapists can model recognizing both the negative and the positive in their statements about what the client reveals about her family, thus increasing the client's tolerance for the reality that the family was neither all good nor all bad. This acknowledgment can help her increase her tolerance for contradictory feelings in general, as well as allow her to continue to benefit from what was good in her family rather than reject everything. In helping clients recognize, when they are ready, that their families were not all bad, timing is crucial. It is not helpful for a therapist to point out the positive in a family when a client is struggling to acknowledge and accept her anger at them. It must be acknowledged that it is not always easy for psychotherapists to hold their own, sometimes intense and sometimes ambivalent, feelings about these families. Frequent supportive supervision or consultation can make this task easier.

Relationships with Teachers

Four participants talked about how their relationships with teachers were important in promoting their school success and providing an antidote to the abuse they were receiving at home. Beth found support from teachers important in helping her achieve academically:

My fourth-grade teacher was pretty significant. She was probably the first teacher to recognize my intelligence, and really encouraged it and fostered it. . . . High school was a bit the same. My life took off academically in high school, and there were teachers who recognized this. . . . At one point my math teacher told me how special he thought I was. And I am now beginning to understand what he was talking about, but I didn't understand it then. And I'm sure that's how I got into [a prestigious women's college], because they all wrote these glowing recommendations.

For Beth and some others, teachers were important largely because they encouraged intellectual development. But for Carrie, female teachers, particularly a college dean, were important role models in her identity development. These models allowed her to modify her identification with her father and become more "woman identified." Having female role models also enabled her to improve her relationship with her mother. "I had other people in my life who filled the needs for a mother figure. . . . I just kind of started to accept [my mother] for who she was."

A particular elementary school teacher played a crucial role in Darlene's life. She described her second-grade teacher:

She's the one who fought to have me tested for [a special accelerated] program, and they had me tested by some woman, I think she was from Germany, with this thick accent. I couldn't understand a word she was saying. I flunked the test, and [the second-grade teacher] fought to have me retested. I aced the test when I had a person who spoke English. She was a white teacher. She really went to bat for me. I overheard the whole thing. I was in the classroom, and she was in the hall yelling at

the principal and someone else to have me retested. I
knew that took a lot. And then also she took me to Sea
World over the summer. So I knew she liked me.

Darlene told us that her participation in this program was essential to her later, impressive academic path. At the time of the initial interviews, she was in the final stages of a doctoral program in
clinical psychology. Darlene also described a number of African
American female teachers who played an important role in promoting her school development: "They used to come to my birth-
day parties and everything." She felt that her relationships with
these teachers were especially corrective for her because she had
been abused by African American women. Her belief, and ours, in
the importance of these relationships to her resiliency is supported
by research carried out by Caren Floyd (1996), who found that resilient African American high school students often describe teachers as having an important role in their school success.

An important aspect of our participants' resiliency was their
ability to attract such benevolent interest from teachers and others,
and then to flourish in the warmth and support of those connections. Psychotherapists should attend to these relationships while
listening to a client's story. The fact that a survivor does well in the
context of a supportive relationship with a teacher augers well for
the likelihood of also doing well in the healing warmth of a therapy relationship. Further, remembered positive connections with
teachers is a good place to begin recognizing the client's resilience in
establishing and being able to receive support in such relationships.
Such therapeutic discussions can help a client see her capacity for
connections, as well as help her recognize when others have been
caring rather than abusive or indifferent. Focus in this area also
draws attention to evidence that others whom she respects found
her worthy of care and attention, an important counter-message to
the one she may have received from her family.

The Meaning of School Success

Most participants talked about the importance of school and their successes in school, but doing well in school meant different things to different women and to their families. One experience our participants discussed was how they were appreciated at school for their abilities. Elena, who had an extraordinary record of achievement in virtually all school activities, talked about how she was "blessed to be very bright" and says, "I just remember feeling known and somewhat special in the school environment." Other researchers (reviewed in Masten and Coatsworth, 1998) have noted that being smart is a powerful resource for resilient survivors.

For most of our participants, excelling in school (and later in work) served as a coping mechanism, a way of escaping from the abuse suffered at home. It was striking how similar their responses to questions about this were and how similarly they described the process. As Darlene said, "I think I put all my stuff into school and I really excelled"—a statement that would be accurate for most of these women. Janet, echoing Darlene, explained: "My schoolwork was real important to me so I never let [the rest of my life] interfere with that. . . . I read a lot. I escaped through reading. And I excelled at schoolwork. I was a workaholic in school, so I think that it got my mind off things. And I just excelled."

Linda Sanford (1992) found that the abuse survivors she spoke with often escaped from intolerable circumstances by focusing on school, frequently forming healthy and affirming relationships with teachers and finding a dependable source of self-esteem.

The success of many of our participants in school had important consequences that extended into their adulthood. As Beth saw with great clarity, the fact that she responded to her painful childhood by turning to books and the pursuit of academic excellence led her to have successes, both in childhood and later, that were instrumental to her survival. Because they focused their energy in this way, rather than, as Beth says, on more self-destructive pursuits, our participants were rewarded with various degrees of worldly success. Most important, their success in school and work enabled many of them to develop their own identities and competencies, to separate from their families, and to have the resources to invest in their recovery. So their success in school reflected both their own and their families' strengths and added significantly to the resources they brought with them into adulthood.

The fact that many of our participants could channel feelings resulting from adverse experiences into success in the academic realm reflects a tremendous ability that demonstrates the essence of resilience. Therapists can help a survivor recognize when she has done this—whether in school, work, or in another realm—thus encouraging the client's ability to see her strengths as well as her weaknesses and supporting the change in the way she views herself.

Resilient Choices

In reviewing our participants' discussion of their lives in school and at work, we noted something remarkable. Often these women made choices related to school or work that later were essential to their recovery. When they made these "resilient" decisions, as we call them now, the women were not aware that their decisions would be essential to their recovery or indeed that there was anything to recover from. An example is the selection of a women's college that turns out to offer a uniquely supportive environment for developing a broader perspective on women's issues, including women's and children's victimization. A number of our participants demonstrated an unconscious sense of what they needed to do for themselves long before they began the conscious process of recovery from abuse.

What was also striking in hearing our participants' responses to our questions was how the school environment often played an important role in initiating the crises that were the beginning of the recovery process. Often, decisions around college offered our participants their first opportunity to make important life decisions for themselves and to break away from their families. Also, going away to college gave some women the space to acknowledge to themselves that something was wrong internally, making it both possible and necessary to begin to address it.

Anne described going to a college that most of her family had attended and being "pretty depressed" and "thinking about committing suicide." She told us, "I would study all the time but I didn't know anything that I read . . . because I didn't understand anything I was doing and I couldn't make the smallest decisions." She went home for Christmas vacation and "had nightmares and waked up screaming and . . . What I understand of it now had to do with separating from my family and getting out from under their control." Ultimately, Anne left that college and, against her parents' wishes, chose a college of her own. In retrospect, that decision "was a good thing because I found a different world, I could be more who I am at [the new college] because nobody knew who I was."

Beth used school to protect herself from her family. She went to boarding school in high school and then realized, during the summer after her sophomore year, that she could not stand to be home anymore. She insisted on going away to summer school and felt that saved her. Similarly, against her mother's wishes, she chose to go out of state to college: "I was bound and determined, after I had gone to boarding school, that I would never go back to [my home state]. And I think that was one thing that really saved me, because my three older sisters, all of them went to college in [my home state] and they have had much more trouble breaking away from the family than I have."

Like several other participants, Darlene used school as a way of avoiding abuse from family members. She told us why she thought the abuse stopped: "I started getting more and more into school and I would tell my mother, 'Oh I can't go [to my aunt's], I have a lot of homework.' Academics became my excuse and my out for a lot of things . . . so [the abuse] just wouldn't happen. I kind of manipulated that situation to try to keep me away from them."

Darlene, like Carrie, chose to attend a women's college even though there was family pressure to attend a prestigious coed school. When she started college, Darlene told us, she was not dealing with her sexual abuse history at all. Then she was exposed to an educational program in her dorm that focused on victimization. She began to think more about the impact the abuse had had on her. Darlene emphasized the importance school has had in her recovery: "Had I been less in school or not as academically able, I feel like I would've been a lot more lost, because I would have had nothing, no resources to fall back on."

Janet also used school as an opportunity to break away from her family, even though (unlike her siblings) she had no financial support from them to do so. However, the unspoken but apparent pleasure her mother took in Janet's academic success—the only pleasure she got from anything Janet did—provided some emotional support for furthering her education. But Janet moved out of her parents' home the day she graduated from high school and went to live with an aunt. She then supported herself through her bachelor's degree at a state university, moved home briefly, and applied to graduate school. When asked how she chose her graduate program, she replied, "I wanted to get far away [laughs]. I did. I wanted to get far away and that was my priority. I applied to all schools that were far away. I got an excellent scholarship. I got paid to go to school." Her move to a different part of the country proved crucial in her ability to break away from her family. Her siblings, however, did not move away geographically and, according to Janet at the time of the initial interviews, had not moved away psychologically either. This process of separating from her family was central to her recovery from abuse.

In this culture, almost all young people need to move away from their families, psychologically if not also geographically, at some point in their path toward adult development. For survivors of abusive families it is even more central. Steve and Sybil Wolin (1993) studied individuals from dysfunctional families and identified a crucial strength underlying resiliency: the ability to sense in childhood that something is wrong with the family, paired with the ability to disengage by adolescence. Virtually all participants talked about some form of moving away from their parents as necessary for recovery, and a surprising number moved away physically very early, sometimes without knowing why the move was necessary.

These participants provide striking examples of how decisions made about one area of life—school—are important indicators of resiliency. Decisions about school were turning points that led to opportunities for positive health and development and for further resilient adaptation. These choices often provided our participants with their first opportunity to move away from the direction their family had specified for them. We can also see these survivors' resilience in their movement away from the role of victim in their families, which boded well for their continued development. Moreover, the path they chose led them in the direction of recovery before they even recognized that they had something to recover from.

The fact that the decision to leave was so often made intuitively raises the question of whether young people generally know what they need, even when they cannot articulate the reasons for it. For example, given the evidence that women's colleges support young women in ways that coeducational settings are less likely to do, we wonder if the several participants who went to women's colleges were not demonstrating some unconscious knowledge of their own needs. The adults advising young people should take this possibility into account, even when doing so does not support the direction that parents, teachers, or other key adults believe best.

Therapists can support a client's self-confidence and trust in her own intuition by helping her see where she has made difficult choices that ended up being turning points or transformative choices. Recovery is not a carefully laid out plan that can be followed like a script. The women we have spoken with did better as they gradually let go of the need for an explicit plan and started to trust that there is a reason for what they do, even though they may not see it at the time. Support from her therapist for this intuition helps a woman begin to build faith in her own internal process of recovery, which is a powerful force for healing.

Our participants' stories also suggest implications for counselors or therapists working with adolescents who are about to go to, or have just entered, college. The transition to college is often a crucial turning point for survivors. Negotiating separation has implications for future adaptation and healing, so giving survivors support can make all the difference in the separation. These supports can include individual therapy, but undoubtedly this population would also benefit from community outreach, which could include psychoeducational programs in residence halls or group therapy around issues of the transition from home and adjustment to school. Many colleges provide such services because this issue is developmentally relevant to their populations. The survivor needs special attention, however, for two reasons: (1) separation from the abusive family is crucial to resilient adaptation, and (2) survivors can have more difficulty accomplishing the separation because of their underlying psychological vulnerability.

We saw in all of our participants that, as much as they needed to obtain and usually maintain distance from their families, they also needed to preserve or rebuild some ties. At the time of the initial interviews, a number of participants wanted more distance from family members, but even then they valued some contact, even if it was painful. As we saw in the follow-up, contact with some family members worked best for most women, although they continued to regulate the nature and amount of that contact.

Therapists can play a crucial role in helping clients regulate family contact. We discourage therapists from suggesting a complete cut-off from families, in part because this is a response to only part of the client's feelings toward her family. If a complete cut-off seems necessary, then the client should be supported in this while the therapist continues to keep open the possibility of later flexibility. Perhaps a cut-off is necessary for a period of time before a healthier reconnection can occur on the survivor's own terms. The therapist's role here, and in trauma work generally, is one of holding all sides of the client's feelings until she can hold them herself. Many clients feel ashamed or confused about wanting reconnection with the family that was abusive. It can help them if they understand that early attachments are extremely sturdy, and there is evidence that traumatic attachments are particularly robust (Blizzard & Bluhm, 1994). Therapists can help clients see the striving for health in their wish for reconnection and help them attend to ways of maintaining some family ties while taking care of themselves emotionally.

With regard to the family of origin, we conclude this section on school by emphasizing three important points. First, despite the evident dysfunction and abusiveness of all of these families, most of our participants got something of value, some strength from their families—often it was support for academic excellence. (Gina Higgins [1994] also found this to be the case in the resilient survivors she interviewed.) The second is that as our participants began to move away from their families in young adulthood, often around their college years, their resiliency began to manifest itself. Last, we are impressed with the durability of their need to maintain ties with members of the original families while maintaining significant distance and establishing firm boundaries. We believe their commitment to hold both sides of this difficult equation is an important aspect of their resiliency.

WORK

Our participants' jobs were different, and they reported different amounts of satisfaction with their jobs. Only one, Felicia, was unemployed at the first of our initial interviews, although she had taken a part-time job by the time of the third. She was on disability but did what amounted to full-time work in a volunteer capacity for a variety of community organizations. Despite their differences all of our participants saw meaningful work as part of their ideal life, and all were invested in their working lives.

Work as Coping

Like school, work has been an area where participants exhibited their resilience. It has provided a context in which they could excel and obtain some respite from the pain in the rest of their lives. Some were particularly enthusiastic about the work they were doing. Anne said, "I love working." She talked about the pleasure she got from teaching music to children: "I love seeing that moment of 'Oh I get it!' whether it's on a three-year-old's face or whether it's a teenager. It's just that whole moment of understanding something. I love challenging them. I just love being with kids, too. They're so refreshing and they're so unencumbered by so many of the adult things! And bringing people along so that they're growing. Whether they're kids or adults. To feed people's esteem, and have them feel good about what they're doing."

For many participants, working had been a productive way of avoiding the more difficult aspects of their lives. As Helen stated, "When I got out of [high] school I worked full-time and I'd have part-time jobs. Always. There was a time when I was working three night-time jobs and full-time waitressing, tent-mending and grocery store. That [work] was a place I hid. I worked and I worked and I worked and I worked. It's incredible."

In this way, work can serve a similar function to school—that of refuge from pain. Therapists should help clients recognize when this is so. Certainly, energy must be spent preserving such a protected place when it is necessary, and vulnerability should be anticipated if it is threatened. Psychotherapists can also help clients attend to when the refuge provides not only a hiding place from pain but an impediment to developing better ways of experiencing, managing, and coping with pain. Survivors may understandably continue to use work—a place that provides them self-esteem, a sense of self-worth and competence—as an escape from the challenge presented by dealing with painful feelings. But they should be encouraged to confront those difficult feelings in due time. Although some of the work may be related to financial need, psychotherapists need to be attentive to the various functions of work in a survivor's life.

The Role of Work in Recovery

The early success that some participants had in school set the stage for a productive working life. Their ability to engage in productive work and succeed at it has been essential for some of these women's recovery. Being able to work enabled them to become independent from their families and support themselves. It is clear that, just as with school, many made resilient choices in the context of their work lives. By resilient choices, we mean those that (whether conscious or not) somehow promoted and secured their recovery.

Beth spoke a great deal about how, although she was not fulfilled by her job, working served a number of important purposes for her. As we said earlier, she knew that her past success in a prestigious M.B.A. program enabled her to gain a position whereby she could both support herself and have the time and resources to focus on her recovery. She described how her job filled a lot of needs at that time. She was well-paid, had regular hours (nine to six), had the flexibility to attend writing classes, and had the time to visit her son and go to therapy. So although Beth was far from satisfied with her job, at the time of the interview it seemed to her and to us an appropriate choice, given what else was going on in her life.

For several participants the context of their work was important in moving them toward engagement in the recovery process. Carrie was working in a halfway house with mentally ill women, many of whom were trauma survivors, when she began to recover memories of her own childhood sexual abuse. She told us that her work with these women played an important role in her recovery process.

When she first began to work there, she had no memories of having been abused. She simply felt herself drawn to the work. Then she found it crucial to her own remembering and therefore, ultimately, healing. As she stated, "In some ways I feel like I've grown with the clients." Similarly, Galen described how working at a battered women's shelter during college caused her to confront her abusive past: "I lived at a shelter and I was the manager, and so I did all the hot lines. I think it was then that I really started to feel [the effects of my traumatic history], because also I wasn't drinking during that time. I started to feel a lot of things and I just really mourned; I started to mourn."

So for Carrie and Galen, working with abused women triggered their confrontation with their own abuse histories. At the time of the initial interviews, both women had chosen to continue to work with abuse survivors and were committed to continuing that work as a way of helping themselves and others.

Psychotherapists working with survivors who have chosen to work with other survivors or in situations that trigger their own traumatic histories should carefully assess with the client whether it is the right time to be doing such work. Therapists can also help clients explore how they have come to find such work and what meaning it has for their own healing. Our participants generally found it furthered their healing work, although they also made choices at times to avoid such triggering experiences. Our intuitive understanding is that more resilient survivors often choose this kind of work when they are ready for it, but a therapist can help clarify the internal work they are addressing when they select such an evocative setting.

In listening to our participants, we realized that choices around work have important implications for recovery. For Beth, working in a job she didn't particularly like but that allowed her to pursue her recovery seemed to be a resilient choice. Working with survivors did trigger memories for Carrie and Galen, thus helping them move through their recovery.

Felicia was unusual in that she was not employed in paid work but was on disability and engaged in extensive volunteer work. At the last initial interview, she told us she had been offered a part-time, paid position. Her volunteer activities, which included community policing and running self-defense programs, as well as sitting on boards of organizations working for gay and lesbian individuals, related in part to her previous career in security and law enforcement. Prior to being disabled, Felicia had excelled as a security officer and had been in the process of qualifying as a police officer. She struggled unsuccessfully to continue working while trying to cope with mental illness and various health problems.

Felicia finally decided to go on disability after a second inpatient hospitalization during which she was advised not to go back to work but to enter a day treatment program. Although she was not making money in the volunteer jobs at the time of the initial interviews, Felicia described her work life as the closest to her ideal it had ever been. She told us why:

> Because sometimes I do have problems; that's why I like this type of work, because I can make my own schedule. And if it is a problem, I can cancel. I made a lot of money as a [security officer], but I was very unhappy. And money is not the issue with me either. It's more that what I'm doing is important for society or the community I'm in. That what's important. Or that I'm getting some sense of creative release; that's important. So I guess, this is the closest I've ever been [to ideal].

So Felicia had made important choices around work that allowed her to get the treatment she needed and gave her the flexibility to limit the amount she worked when she started to feel stressed and distressed. She was still able to find fulfillment in being creative and giving to the community.

In general, therapists should work with clients to explore the ways their work choices or aspirations may be supportive of their recovery. Resiliency can be seen in the way survivors choose triggering or nontriggering settings and in their choices for financial security or for emotional benefits such as self-esteem. Some survivors may be self-critical for not doing exactly what they aspire to; they suffer from a chronic "not good enough" feeling. It often takes an outside perspective for a woman survivor to notice and appreciate the ways she is taking care of herself in her work.

Conflicts at Work

Although work was an area of success for most of our participants, many found that unresolved issues with their families came up in relation to people at work, requiring them to do further work on these old and new conflicts. Galen, Helen, and Janet spoke the most about how these issues caused them difficulty in their work lives. All three described difficulty dealing with authority that they related to their histories of abuse by their parents. Helen described this connection most vividly: "He [my boss] reminds me of my father and she [my other boss] reminds me of my mother, so I have this constant battle with it pretty much in my head a lot: "She's not my mother, she's not my mother, he's not my father. He might treat me like he's my father, but he's not my father."

Thus, Helen talked to herself as a way to calm down when she found the conflicts in her family of origin were being triggered at work. Her resilience was expressed in her ability to recognize triggers (interactions with authority) and cope with them in a way that allowed her to stay in her job. She also took these issues to her therapy and was working hard to understand and deal with them more successfully.

The difficulties our participants had with authority at work included dealing with conflict, assertiveness, and triggers caused by someone in power. Galen described what it was like for her: "I am afraid that connection with anger and violence in my mind is still lurking; even though I've tried to let go of it, I still have some. And expressing anger toward an authority figure especially is really really hard for me, like my boss at work . . . I feel so angry at her, but I don't feel like I can express it at her. And I feel really sometimes submissive in bringing things up."

In spite of these difficulties Galen told us that having to deal with authority at work had been helpful to her recovery. At one of her jobs, authority issues came up, but her boss was able to work with her on them. She described this process, saying that at the residential treatment setting where she worked, "they say people teach most what they want to learn themselves and I felt that was really true for me there, because I taught . . . conflicts come up between people near you and that it's OK that people get angry, and it's all right; it's not going to lead to abuse. I would have conflicts with [my bosses] and I would feel comfortable with the differences between us and being able to talk with them, and try to work with them, even though it would be hard."

It was important for Galen's recovery that these conflicts come up but that she be able to work through them. Obviously, having a supportive work context allowed her to do this.

Janet, in particular, went through a number of jobs because of issues with supervisors. From her account, she started her own private practice of psychotherapy because she was unable to resolve these issues in her work setting:

> I had a lot of jobs. That's why I have my own practice now. Because I couldn't stand working for other people. I would end up usually in some kind of conflict. Not all of the time but a lot of the time I worked for the wrong people. I'm sure I was acting out my issues in the workplace. Now I work the way I want, and I don't have a conflict. And I have a peer supervision group of people that I want to be in contact with.

We see this as a resilient solution to what had been a difficult and ongoing problem. She was much happier with her work once she made the change.

So even experiences that could be viewed as negative, such as conflicts at work, become grist for the mill for resilient survivors and can become important sources of new learning and recovery. Part of the therapist's job is to help the survivor remember past successes in resolving conflicts in work or other settings and to remind her of what an important source of learning such conflicts can offer.

Stability in the realm of work supports both financial and emotional independence. By working, the survivor can afford necessary resources for education and therapy—investments in healing the sense of self that was damaged by abuse. Financial independence also facilitates the survivor leaving an abusive home or partner, thereby creating a safer emotional space in which she can do the work of healing. Helping the survivor appreciate the value of a stable foundation in school and work is one of the most important tasks of the beginning stages of therapy with people with histories of abuse.

4

Intimate Relationships

One of the greatest difficulties that adult survivors of childhood familial abuse have is building healthy, reciprocal, intimate relationships. Because the abuse occurred originally in the context of family, the survivors' first experiences of close connections were distorted and perverted, to varying degrees. Despite the all-too-evident difficulties survivors have in this area of their lives, however, many do show resiliency. In this chapter we describe three important areas of strength in the intimate partnerships of many of our participants and the ways psychotherapists can work with these potential resources in their clients.

First, despite the great pain and dysfunction in some of their earliest important relationships, which can discourage some children from allowing anyone to get close again, all of the women in our study showed a courageous commitment to having good intimate ties. They also showed a determination to work hard over many years to attain those ties. Second, at the time of the first or follow-up interviews, many had established enduring and satisfying intimate partnerships. The third point we wish to emphasize is the extent to which a number of our participants, even when they were quite young and often unaware of their abusive histories, showed their resiliency by either avoiding abusive relationships with partners or by getting out of such relationships quickly once begun.

At the time of the initial interviews a number of our participants were in marriages or committed relationships; four were lesbian and six heterosexual.

A DETERMINATION
TO HAVE INTIMATE TIES

All of our participants showed their determination to be in satisfying and reciprocal relationships, even though they were at different stages of that process at the time of the initial interviews. For Felicia and Helen, intimacy was still extremely threatening, but they were committed to healing and developing until they could have good intimate partnerships. Both described themselves as having no close ties throughout their childhood, no one they could trust or turn to, which makes their determination even more remarkable.

To focus briefly on Felicia's narrative, at the time of the initial interviews she was in a committed lesbian relationship of over a year's duration. She and her partner, Marge, each had her own apartment but took turns staying with each other; they shared a cat. Felicia had learned to set boundaries with Marge and negotiate, especially around having her own separate time and space. She said, "I don't like too much closeness; I feel smothered, and then I just want to run again. And I think she feels that too." Having a shared cat and separate apartments strikes us as a creative way to negotiate issues of closeness and distance, which are often so difficult for survivors. Therapists can help clients by acknowledging and making legitimate their need for boundaries and separate space, as well as their need for sharing and intimacy.

There had been several somewhat violent incidents between Felicia and Marge, but they were working hard to find alternative ways of communicating. Felicia was very much aware of her own difficulties in allowing intimacy: "I don't ever feel close to anyone really. I mean I do feel close to Marge, and I'm learning each year more and more how to be a better mate and how to expect more, too, from a person who's going to be my mate." She told us at the initial interviews that she would rate her relationship with her partner at about 5 on a 10-point scale but said with determination and conviction, "I'm gonna say I'm all right here, and I'm gonna get better, and when I get to 10, I'll get there. But I'm not there."

Although we, like Felicia, see clearly the effects of her traumatic history on her intimate relationships, we also see her resiliency. Central to her resiliency was her determination to have a good intimate tie, her belief that such a connection was possible for her, and her willingness to work on herself and with her partner until she got there. It is important for therapists and clients to notice and celebrate when survivors' awful experiences in connections in childhood do not lead them away from relationships, as can happen for some traumatized children. Maintaining such an emphasis in therapy helps sustain a balance for both therapists and clients between the sometimes painfully slow work of improving the way survivors go about seeking intimacy and an appreciation of the powerful and life-sustaining motivation that propels them to keep trying.

We think therapists can also help clients like Felicia appreciate some of the early evidence of their strengths, which become sources of their later resiliency. We would help someone like Felicia see the strength in her ability, even as a young child, to perceive the world from a broader perspective, to understand, as she told us she did at age nine after reading a book about world philosophy, that there were ways to understand and live in the world other than the ways her family had shown her. We would emphasize that being a very smart girl helped her reach this understanding and that another important source of her later strength was her spirituality. Finally, we would talk with her about the strength she got from knowing, when she was a child, that she was cherished by her grandmother and that she had had two and a half good years living with her aunt after her father kidnapped her from her mother's house. When therapists help put the sources of a client's resiliency into perspective, clients can see themselves more accurately and appreciate what they did get, without minimizing the negatives of their history.

Anne had struggled for many years with a difficult marriage. When we met Anne she was forty-five and had been married for twenty-three years to James, whom she had dated since she was fifteen. The marriage was problematic for Anne. For years James had been irrationally concerned that she was "dressing like a whore" and showing her body to other men. He had a serious problem with drinking. There had been several instances of physical violence. His emotional abuse was a constant for all of the earlier years of their marriage. As Anne progressed in her recovery she became increasingly aware of how frustrating, enraging, and inappropriate his behavior was. She knew she was not ready to leave him because she could not support herself and her four children, either financially or psychologically.

We view Anne's story as an example of the perseverance of resilient survivors in working toward healthy intimacy. Despite steady opposition from her husband, she continued to work on her ability to keep her voice in her marriage, to honor her own needs and wishes, and to value herself. At the first set of interviews she told us there were many leisure activities she would have liked to do but hadn't because her husband did not want to. But things were changing:

> Again, as I've gotten older and healthier, I've just, well, I'm just going to do it. And I'll say things like, "I'm getting tickets to see XYZ, do you want to come?" He gets furious, because he says I should be asking him if he wants to see XYZ; I shouldn't say I'm going whether you're going or not. And my therapist says he'll calm down after a few days, and he'll either say he's going or he's not. But you can't not do everything in your life that you want to because you're fearful of his rage. And I guess I've gotten better at that but it's still real painful, and it's something that takes enormous energy.

Psychotherapists can help clients in less-than-ideal relationships find ways to continue to grow by acknowledging the real-life difficulties that keep people in problematic relationships and appreciating the strength of clients who continue to develop their voice in the face of opposition.

THE DEVELOPMENT OF STRONG INTIMATE RELATIONSHIPS

Several of our participants surprised us by the quality of their intimate partnerships. In some ways Ilona's marriage is the most remarkable, not because it was a marriage made in heaven but because it survived and had genuine strengths. Ilona had grown up living alone in hotel rooms and being sexually abused or living with strangers or uncaring relatives and being abused. She was married briefly and had a daughter before her husband died. Several years later she married Aaron, her husband at the time of the initial interviews. Although she told us she had not loved Aaron when she married him, she had done so because he "always had time for [my daughter]," and "I felt that if I didn't do something that I was going to wind up as [my mother] did. Revolving door, succession of men in my life. And I was bound and determined that the buck was going to stop with me." Here Ilona illustrates the way many survivors can change their lives for the better if they feel the change is helping their children. Therapists can use that motivation to encourage their clients to tolerate the process of change and the pain that trauma therapy evokes.

According to Ilona, when she began to change, initially through her experiences at Overeaters Anonymous where she learned how she was using food to soothe her feelings, the couple began to have more problems. Although Aaron had resisted her changes, leading to volatile and spectacular fights for a number of years, they stayed together and raised two children. She told us she had needed to teach him about respecting boundaries, which she had learned at

Overeaters Anonymous and later in psychotherapy. Ilona struggled more with her marriage than some of our other participants because it had been established for such a long time before she began her recovery. We find it impressive that she and Aaron were able to keep the marriage together through this process, which is often extremely difficult for couples. Working with clients like Ilona, it is essential for therapists to be mindful of the particulars of the client's history as a context for discussions about relationships. Thus we see Ilona showing remarkable resiliency in her marriage to Aaron, in the context of her history, even though we might have quite different responses to another client with a different history. It is important to show clients how to find their own strengths, both to help counteract the extreme shame and self-denigration so many carry and to help them find ways to use those strengths in their continuing recovery. With a client like Ilona, we (and she) might wonder what aspects of herself made it possible for her to stay with Aaron and continue to work on their relationship. We might also wonder whether that part of herself might help in other struggles. It is possible that some part of Ilona is particularly tenacious and has learned to persevere despite discouragement and pain. Might that part be called up to help when she despairs over her nightmares and flashbacks?

At the time of the initial interviews Ilona was very positive about her marriage. "He has always been there, and he's always taken care of me." She said she had grown to love Aaron dearly. "It's a relationship that's evolved over the years. We've both grown." For all of their obvious difficulties, it seems little short of miraculous that the little girl who grew up alone in a hotel room, neglected by her parents and seriously abused by others was able to have a stable and in many ways supportive marriage for over thirty-five years.

As with Felicia we would help Ilona understand more about the source of her amazing resiliency. She has impressive grit and determination. She told us that the buck was going to stop with her; she was determined to stop the "revolving door" sequence of relationships with men that had been her mother's life. She was, and is, a very determined woman. We don't know exactly what moved her to go to Overeater's Anonymous, beyond the fact that she was struggling with obesity, but once there, she recognized it for the lifesaver it turned out to be and used it not just to lose weight but to begin to recover from her traumatic childhood.

We hope any therapist working with a survivor like Ilona would recognize and celebrate such resiliency. We also hope this book will help therapists be sensitive to more subtle signs of such strength in less obviously resilient survivors. In no way should such a focus limit therapists' freedom to continue to explore areas of vulnerability.

Elena is a survivor with a strong intimate tie that has also become even richer and more satisfying with her (and her partner's) continuing growth. At the time of the initial interviews, Elena was living in a committed lesbian relationship of three years. She and Claire had recently bought a house together. Part of what moved Elena about their connection was that Claire was very responsive to a child part of Elena that she had gotten to know during her process of recovery. Elena said, "I've never been happier. I can only imagine it will continue to get better. I love her more than I ever knew I could love anyone, and just truly daily, if not many times during the day, I feel infinitely blessed about my life, and she's a major part of it."

Intimacy had not always been easy for her. She had struggled for a number of years before she could use her voice in relationships. However, as early as high school, Elena was aware of needing to work on this issue and started on a trajectory of becoming more able to assert herself, which would ultimately be central to her recovery. She had also struggled with not being able to allow someone else to love her until, in an early intimate relationship, she said, "I allowed myself to feel that [early partner] loved me, so I got a sense of what I was missing, and so when that relationship ended, I think I have this desire to be able to do more. It was finally almost safe enough in my life that maybe I ought to be able to do it."

Five years later, she told us about the strength and ever-growing richness of her relationship with Claire. They had a formal wedding, at which many family members from both sides participated, and by all accounts their partnership flourished. Besides helping a client like Elena appreciate the strength in her long-term and successful striving for a satisfying, committed relationship, a therapist would also focus on the particular strengths that led to this capacity—strengths that can be applied to other areas in which the client may still be struggling.

AVOIDING ABUSIVE RELATIONSHIPS

Many survivors of childhood sexual abuse find themselves repeating abusive and destructive relationships in adolescence and adulthood. We were impressed that at the time of the initial interviews, none of our participants were in physically abusive relationships, and only a few were in psychologically or emotionally abusive partnerships. In fact, many told us stories about somehow knowing enough to stay away from or get out of abusive connections, even when they were quite young. Darlene was always able to avoid abusive intimate ties, despite having grown up surrounded by abuse.

Historically, she told us, she had always been able to maintain her safety in intimate relationships. She had never been in a sexually or physically abusive intimate relationship. When one lesbian lover tried to do something to her that Darlene had asked her not to do, she said, "I dumped her, because I felt like she wasn't respecting what I wanted." Not only did she successfully avoid physically abusive ties but she was aware of what she needed to say and do around emotional connections. She told us she needed to talk through issues in any close connection, and that was true in nonintimate as well as intimate relationships, although "a little more heated" in the latter: "I have this thing where I can't keep stuff. If people are going to be actively involved in my life, I can't keep feelings under cover, or minimize. It's like I have to get it out; I have to say what I have to say." She was sometimes quick tempered, she said, and could be sharp tongued, but it always got worked out. "I think I try very hard to have my love relationships very different than my familial relationships, because I didn't want to repeat the same kind of stuff—colluding with violence and keeping feelings in the closet."

Darlene felt that her abuse at the hands of black women made it harder for her to trust black women as partners, and she struggled with that. We understand that the trust issue was a large one for her. However, we were impressed with her ability to represent her truths in relationships and to maintain her safety and see both of these abilities as strongly reflective of her resilience. For example, for her to avoid abusive relationships, she needed to have an impressive perceptiveness about who is likely to be dangerous. Clients with such awareness are often not aware that they have this clarity. When therapists help them see that strength in themselves, they can feel more confident of being able to recognize risk when it confronts them, which can allow them access to more awareness of all their thoughts and feelings. A therapist for a client like Darlene can help her understand the sources of her resiliency.

Galen learned in early adulthood to avoid abusive relationships. During the period covered by our first several interviews, Galen was in a good relationship, but she told us she had gone through what she called a promiscuous period shortly after she came out as a lesbian, during which she was also drinking heavily. (Addictions are often used by survivors to cope with intolerable feelings, particularly to mask feelings. Unfortunately, helpful feelings are also distorted and masked. The survivor then loses her ability to be attuned to her own feelings. Therapists should not expect clients to establish healthy intimacy while active in addictions.) She said, "I slept with tons and tons of women." And she said, "I just didn't have very good boundaries so I was raped a couple of times by women." She continued to get involved in abusive relationships until she came to realize that she was a survivor of sexual abuse. That was a crucial realization for her. "I put everything together, and I realized I wasn't to blame for what was going on with me; I wasn't crazy, that this is why . . . everything made sense. I read an article in *Lesbian Psychology* about lesbian survivors and put a lot of things together, and that's when I broke up with this woman. It was really hard to break up with her, to get away from her, and that's when I chose sobriety and cleaned my slate up."

Galen's vulnerabilities around intimacy are evident, but she has surprising areas of strength. Although she had fears of being violent in relationships, as her father had been, she avoided going in that direction. When she understood that she had a traumatic history that was driving her unsafe sexual behavior, she got out of an abusive relationship and moved toward sobriety—two difficult feats. Fundamental to establishing healthy intimacy is increasing self-awareness about past relationships and about feelings in the present. Knowledge about past relationships is important so that unhealthy relationship patterns are not merely repeated self-destructively. One of the most important tasks of therapists working with incest survivors is to help clients understand the impact of past relationships while celebrating the client's ability to see that she can choose and create relationships that are very different from those she knew growing up. Knowledge of feelings in the present is important because feelings provide data that can be used to keep one safe and protect one's own needs and interests in a relationship.

Psychotherapy plays a central role in facilitating the development of satisfying and reciprocal intimate relationships. Survivors of serious childhood sexual abuse are able to have such relationships, and psychotherapy is one major intervention that makes it possible.

5

Relationships with Children

W e know that most people who have been abused in child-hood do not, as adults, abuse their own or other people's children. Yet even survivors who do not become perpetrators often bring into the next generation problems in parenting that stem from the serious disturbances in their own upbringing (Bar-On, 1995; Thompson & Calkins, 1996). Our participants provided us with a rich opportunity to learn how their parenting had gone and to focus on how they had manifested and then avoided transmitting inter-generational problems.

We emphasize four points in this chapter. First, the women in our study have shown a strong commitment to being better parents than their own parents were. Second, several of these mothers have intuitively understood that openness (instead of secrecy) is very important in raising healthy children. Third, the extra worry that survivors exhibit about their children's healthy development can be interpreted as a potential strength, which can be a valuable focus for a therapist. Fourth, the timing of having children within a recovery process has an impact on a survivor's relationships with her children. Throughout, we suggest ways therapists can respond to clients who are survivors and who have children—responses that capitalize on survivors' strengths.

Four of the participants—Janet, Ilona, Beth, and Anne—had children. The context of each of their lives was very different, particularly because of the differences in their ages and in the ages of their children.

A STRONG COMMITMENT
TO BETTER PARENTING

All four of these women cared deeply about providing better parenting to their children than they had received, and each was determined to act differently in particular areas. When we interviewed her, Janet's children were four and two. Four-year-old Rebecca was a gregarious preschooler with many friends, and two-year-old Mathew was a handful but seemed to be doing all right. Janet enjoyed her children a great deal; she was surprised at how special the experience of parenting was to her. "I'd say it's better than I ever thought it would be. . . . You give a lot but you really get back a lot. . . . It's absolutely better than I ever would have thought it would be. . . . It's harder than I ever thought it would be; I never knew how hard it was, but it's the most satisfying."

Although the children were young when we first talked with her, Janet had been able to establish a loving and supportive home for them that felt different in important ways from the one in which she grew up. Janet, like many parents, whether from abusive families or not, was determined to do some things differently. Given the extreme and repeated physical violence in her family of origin, Janet was particularly concerned that there be no physical violence toward her children. She told us with emphasis, "No, I will not hit the kids. [My husband] will not hit the kids. No. We don't hit our kids. I mean there've been times when I've come close and I felt like it but. . . . No. And we tell them we won't. Rachel didn't even know what spanking was. We were reading something and it had 'spanking' in it, and she had no clue what that was. That will not be a form of discipline."

We appreciate her commitment to nonviolent means of discipline and have no doubt that her children are much the better for it. A therapist working with such a client should remind her of this important attainment. In her determination to raise children differently, she had moved away from physical violence toward them but was not yet able to move away from a strong internal focus on issues of violence and discipline in child rearing. It is often true that parents can avoid precise repetitions of dysfunctional behaviors, but the issue is still an organizing theme. That also can change during the course of recovery, as therapists gradually and without shaming their clients help them see the way their parenting is organized around old themes and help them find alternatives.

Jon was nine at the time we first interviewed Beth and, since a custody trial four years before, had been living with his father in a different part of the country. At that time, Beth was spending as much time with him as she was allowed—one weekend a month and three months during holiday or summer vacation times. She spoke with him on the phone several times a week, sent him small packages frequently, and talked to his teachers regularly. Mother and son had a very strong relationship, and at that time it seemed to Beth and to us that Jon was doing very well.

Jon was of central importance to Beth. Although she had built an impressive career with her M.B.A. and high-level position at a prestigious academic institution, her relationship with her son was the most important thing in her life. For Beth, the custody decision was awful, one of the worst things that could have happened to her, and in psychotherapy she was forced to do a great deal of work to come to terms with the intense pain, loss, and guilt it created. At the time of the trial she had had a sophisticated understanding of the social and political issues that influence custody decisions— issues such as that society (represented by judges) tends to disapprove of women who choose to leave their marriages (which she had done), that her ex-husband had been better able financially to carry out the custody fight, and that her therapist's notes would be subpoenaed and used against her. Nonetheless, the pain, shame, stigmatization, and loss of a sense of identity as a mother were overwhelming to her for several years.

Despite all the difficulties of long-distance mothering of a young child and of a former husband who blocked her relationship with their son at every opportunity, Beth held strong views and high standards about what constituted good parenting; she carried those out with Jon. She believed strongly that Jon should not get caught in the conflict between her and the boy's father and did a variety of things to protect him. She told us that when Jon complains about his father, "I'll say, 'OK, let's talk about all the things you like about your dad. Yeah, he's got this stuff he's not so good at but what about the stuff you like? . . . I'm not perfect at it, but I try real hard to have Jon realize he needs to love; he loves his dad and his dad's important to him. That's good for Jon's life."

Like Janet, Beth was deeply committed to being a better parent than her own parents had been. We see her doing just that with Jon. Besides validating her for this, a therapist might fruitfully work with Beth to help her understand the source of her strengths in this arena. We might wonder, with someone like Beth, whether her ability to relate lovingly and well to Jon despite her loss of custody came, in part, from the resiliency she developed in the face of her childhood abuse. As a resilient child she had learned to develop and in some ways thrive despite awful life circumstances. Skills honed in that crucible may have allowed her to function better than many parents would have after losing custody of a child for whom they had been the primary caretaker.

Anne, in a difficult marriage of many years standing, also cared deeply about the quality of her parenting. At the time of the interviews, her four children were adolescents and were generally doing well. Although there had been some difficult times in Anne's relationship with her children, she loved and admired them and had a close relationship with each of them. She gave many examples of their strong connections and of their wonderful, shared sense of humor. In spite of what she described as the father's nonresponsiveness to the children and his drinking problem, she had worked hard to give her children good parenting and had been remarkably successful. When therapists view their clients' parenting skills, it is crucial that they remember the context of the parenting and remind themselves and their clients of what their clients are doing well rather than focus exclusively on problems.

Ilona was the oldest participant and also had the oldest children—a daughter, Michele, who was then thirty-eight, and Michael, who was then thirty-four and the father of three sons. They lived far away. By the time Ilona began to work on issues from her history, the children were in their twenties, so it was late for them to gain much benefit from the lessons Ilona learned about not passing on issues of abuse and neglect. Stories she told us about her early interactions with her children were painful to hear, as she described behaving destructively and, at times, abusively. Her relationships with her children at the time of the initial interviews were complex and problematic. She talked about loving Michael but not liking him or being able to accept his various addictions. She relied heavily on emotional support from Michele but at times would erupt in rage at her. Nonetheless, despite her horrifying family history and many difficulties she had with her children, over the years Ilona had shown an impressive, powerful motivation to create a more stable family life, and she had been successful. Furthermore, despite all of the earlier difficulties, at the follow-up interview we noticed, in Ilona's relationship with both of her children, constructive changes that were extremely important to all of them. Michael had come for his first visit with his sons, and they had had a wonderful time getting acquainted or reacquainted. Ilona told us with tears in her eyes that she felt, for the first time, able to completely accept Michael for who he was. She loved the experience of being a grandmother to his children, who had responded to her very positively. With Michele, Ilona had set firm limits on financial assistance and backed up her words with action.

Although it had been difficult and Ilona feared Michele would sever their connection over it, that had not occurred and their relationship seemed to be on a healthier track.

We are impressed with both Ilona's and her children's continuing ability to change and grow and the importance of such changes to all of them. With clients like Ilona, with her history of growing up alone in hotel rooms, terribly neglected, and sexually abused by a variety of people, holding the historical context of her parenting would be a vitally important part of the therapist's job in supporting her through the work on her parenting.

One way these women showed resiliency was in their hopes and efforts to be better parents than their own parents had been and their success in doing so. For example, none of the mothers in our sample had abused their children sexually, and three had been able to avoid physical or emotional abuse. Therapists have the important job of witnessing survivors' sometimes heroic efforts to avoid passing on some of the dysfunction of the previous generation. By doing this job well, therapists support and encourage their clients in their continued efforts to relate to their children in healthier ways.

THE IMPORTANCE OF OPENNESS IN SURVIVORS' FAMILIES

We noticed that several participants who are mothers sense the importance of finding ways to be open with their children about matters of ongoing family life, as well as about their abuse histories. In an important study of second- and third-generation Holocaust survivors, Israeli psychologist Dan Bar-On (1995) describes three ways that trauma is passed on from parents to the next generation: in the explicit telling of the story, in the actions of an earlier generation that the next generation models or avoids, and through unprocessed feelings that have not been told in words. In his view, the third has the most impact, which we suspect is due to the central importance of words in understanding and processing feelings. Faye Snider

(1994) makes a similar point in writing about her clinical work with second- and third-generation Holocaust survivors. She gives many examples of children in such families who "know" their parents' stories in some deep and emotional way, whether or not they can articulate what they know, and whether or not they have been told in words. This is a rich and thought-provoking formulation that has potential value in understanding the intergenerational transmission of trauma in incest survivors. We think children do know if their parents have been traumatized, and they absorb unconsciously many of the associated images, thoughts, feelings, and symptoms such as irrational fears or obsessional thoughts. Being given the words lends structure and clarity to what otherwise are confusing, inchoate somatic and psychological experiences that are the residue of often unconscious transmissions by their parents. The importance of this concept made us particularly curious to learn what our participants thought about telling their stories to their children and what they had confided thus far. For survivors whose families' dysfunction had been clothed in secrecy and silence, their commitment to openness reflects their resilience.

Because of the secrecy that had been so destructive to her family, Beth was determined that there would be no secrets in her relationship with Jon. He let her know when he was angry, she said, "because he knows he can be angry at me and I'll still love him, and I'll help him work through the anger." Her openness with him is unusual and admirable. "I tell him when I'm mad at the judge or I'm sad, and I think that's important that it not be kept secret. . . . I feel a lot of shame that I don't have custody of my son, but I think it's important to talk about that shame and how I wish I had done it differently."

At the follow-up interview when Jon was fifteen, Beth said she had told him a little about her abuse history and believed he understood that he could ask more when he was ready to hear it. Given the degree of openness she had fostered between herself and Jon, we suspect that she is right that he feels he has permission to ask.

We also support her decision to let him have some control of the timing of further discussion.

An important job of therapists working with survivor clients is to help them arrive at appropriate expectations of their children at different ages and stages, because usually the view of what children can do and what they should be asked to do was distorted in their families of origin. For example, they may need help seeing that a six-year-old should not be asked to hear about his mother's depression or loneliness, even though in the survivor's original family she may have been asked to provide this kind of support when she was two years old.

Anne also particularly valued openness with her children. In that context, we asked at the follow-up interview what she had told them about her history of physical, sexual, and emotional abuse. She said they knew the way her mother was totally lacking in respect for other people's boundaries because she had behaved that way around them. She said she had not told them about the sexual abuse because she did not want to burden them with it, then said she thought maybe she had talked with one or more of them about it, then again said she wasn't sure. We were struck by this lack of clarity in Anne, a logical and articulate woman. Her confusion could have come from her own ambivalence about whether telling her story to her children would burden them or clarify things for them. Because at the follow-up interview Anne's children were late adolescents or young adults, we thought it in their best interest to understand more of their mother's abuse history. In the process of family life, her history became, in subtle and important ways, a part of their own histories.

However, with clients like Anne, who continued to be ambivalent about what and how to tell, we suggest that therapists work slowly and cautiously, first exploring what it might mean to tell the children. Only as the client is ready is it useful to focus on the particulars of what to tell and how to tell it.

In the follow-up interview Janet said that in the context of her having a very strong reaction to taking a course in Model Mugging, her husband had said something to their young children about her having been treated badly by her parents when she was young. She felt that their knowing a little about her story was helpful in her relationship with them, particularly to her daughter Rebecca who, at age nine, was very attentive to her mother's moods and pain. Rebecca had then started asking more questions about the nature and extent of Janet's physical abuse, and Janet answered her questions as she asked them. Although talking openly about the abuse made her somewhat uncomfortable, Janet was clear that she and her husband would respond to the children's questions. Janet had the advantage of effective trauma therapy before she had children, and it shows in her responses to them.

In general, then, we saw resiliency in several participants' commitment to being more open about important family matters than their own parents had been. In particular, we suggest that more of the destructive effects of a parent's traumatic history are conveyed when the experience is not put into words than when it is. Therapists can help clients consider when and how to tell children about their painful histories. In planning this process, the therapist can help weigh not only the child's readiness but the parent's readiness as well. Telling about abuse can be disorganizing emotionally and cognitively. A disorganized parent is a frightening parent, particularly for young children. A survivor has to get to a place in her recovery from which she can tell a version of her story in a way that is contained and not overwhelming for her or the child. Telling can be a goal, but its usefulness should be weighed against its potential destructiveness. Our participants' caution suggests that they may be aware of this. Making it clear to children that there is something to know about a parent's history and that the topic is open for conversation and questions, just as other important topics are open, is a good way of broaching the topic. Children often sense when they are ready for information, especially difficult and painful knowledge. When given permission and some framework, they often seek it when they are ready. We do not advocate sitting down with a young child, or even an adolescent, and saying, "I have a story to tell you" and then providing an autobiography. But children ultimately need to know in a coherent and organized way what they already know intuitively.

WORRYING CAN BE A GOOD THING

Many childhood abuse survivors worry a lot about the well-being of their children. Although most parents worry, the intensity and the particular shape of survivors' worries are greatly colored by their history. We saw that in all of the mothers in our sample. For example, at the time of the first interviews Janet was worrying a great deal about her son. When we first talked with her, she thought he was doing well but she did have some concerns. "He's very strong willed, and he's a two-year-old. He has difficulty obviously sharing and all that. He's just a normal, I think he's a normal two-year-old, more on the aggressive side than not. He has aggressive tendencies at his toddler program at school. But it's not off the meter [sighs]. It's just that he's very strong willed."

Janet was particularly concerned, given her original family's history of uncontrolled aggression. In some ways that worry was a burden in her child rearing. At the follow-up she told us that shortly after the initial interviews Mathew had been diagnosed as having attention deficit hyperactivity disorder (ADHD), and since then had benefited from many therapeutic and preventive programs she had found—a special preschool program with an emphasis on teaching socialization, tutoring in kindergarten and first grade, therapy, and others. As a result, by age seven he was working up to grade level academically, faring better with friendships, and feeling better about himself. Janet told us she had come to realize that her younger brother, who had been so physically abused by their father for his behavior, almost certainly had ADHD, and she thought other people in her family might have it as well. She talked with justifiable satisfaction about how it felt to handle such a child in a supportive and loving way, giving him the assistance he needed very early in his development—in contrast to the way her family had handled it. So here again, as with her concern about Rebecca, her worry about Mathew led to a very early diagnosis and consequently to early and successful treatment for him.

We suggest that therapists help reframe what might appear to be their clients' excessive worry about their children and focus on the positive side of it: their clients' vigilance in making sure their children are well nurtured and protected. Although therapists may need to help clients give their children freedom from extreme parental concern, clients are more apt to receive this message if they also hear about ways they are doing well with the complex job of parenting.

Beth worried about Jon, both because of his forced separation from her and, we suspect, because of her own history of trauma in her family. When he got depressed a year after the custody trial, she noticed his depression and was determined to do something about it. She insisted he see a psychiatrist, who helped him process his feelings about the divorce and custody trial. Some years later he told his mother that therapy had been helpful. We believe that her tendency to worry about him led her to notice, earlier than many parents might, how distressed he was and to take effective action. A therapist with a client like Beth should communicate that positive fact to the client.

In a variety of ways Anne expressed concerns about her children. One of the positive legacies of her history and treatment experiences was a sometimes impressive degree of self-awareness and honesty in the way she considered her children's lives. Reflecting her ongoing concerns, she said, "I describe my children. They're wonderful, but who knows how they feel about it all. And about their father's drinking or [my relationship with my husband] . . . They feel responsible and I'm sure they're going to have fallout from all of that." And she said that, ironically, her mother had taken child psychology courses in order not to repeat with her children (Anne and her sisters) what had happened to her. Yet Anne knew her mother still did some awful things. "So there is that awful fear, What am I doing? And the jury is still out." And even though we expect there will be fallout from her and her husband's problematic histories and from her husband's drinking, we are convinced that the children are significantly better off because of Anne's work in recovery and because of her concerns about her children.

Survivors tend to see only the negative side of their thoughts and feelings and are likely to be critical of themselves for worrying so much. A vital role for therapists is to notice these actual and potential strengths and to help their clients see them as well. Beyond that, therapists can help clients sort out for themselves when their worrying is probably caught in old and unhelpful pathways and when it might well be in response to something real, but subtle, that needs to be attended to in their children.

THE TIMING OF HAVING CHILDREN

We were fortunate that the four women in our sample who had children spanned a wide range of ages and stages, allowing us to explore the similarities and differences in their relationships as they related to stages of recovery. The fact that Janet had spent some years in recovery before having her children undoubtedly was helpful. Given the neglect and abuse in Janet's childhood, it seems remarkable to us that she was doing as well with her young family as she was. Neither we nor Janet doubt that issues related to her abuse history will periodically arise in connection with her parenting, but we are confident that she will obtain and make effective use of appropriate help.

Beth told us that the loss of custody of her four-year-old son was so difficult that it forced her to grow and learn in ways she would not have without the loss. As she said, "I think if I hadn't suffered the loss of Jon in the custody battle, I probably wouldn't have learned how to grieve." The ability to grieve was what gave her the inner strength to begin to remember and process her history of childhood abuse. And although Beth did not say much about it, we suspect that those years of therapy when Jon was very young helped her establish the good relationship she had with him at the time of the initial interviews.

There's no doubt that Anne's work in therapy to come to terms with her abusive history helped her respond well to her children. For example, she told us that she had learned to say, "Talk to your father," when the children raised issues about their father, such as his drinking. She enjoyed the openness between herself and her children but was mindful that some boundaries needed to be maintained. "I have to be careful that I don't use them just to make me feel better about it. . . . You know there is a fine line between sharing things with them in order to exonerate me or to free me of all the guilt." Her efforts to maintain good boundaries are remarkable for a woman who grew up in a family where so few boundaries were honored.

That Ilona did not begin her recovery until her children were in their twenties made their relationships in childhood more difficult. Although she was able to establish a stable home for them, she was at times physically violent, and she threatened violence toward her husband and children. Once she had done significant work on her recovery, she could respond differently to her children. She told us of a recent example. Michael, who had struggled with substance abuse, confided in her that he had been sexually abused by a doctor in childhood and then by some older boys. As he was talking to her, she knew he was drinking. "I also heard the ice tinkling in the glass [chuckles] as he was talking, and I heard the sips being taken as he was talking, and I thought, 'Well, OK if that's what it takes,' you know, 'to get him to open up. Then that's what it takes.' But that's really something to have a man share with his mother. And I knew that it was special."

Rather than focus critically on his drinking, as she might have in the past, she knew it was important to be responsive to this confidence. "What I really tried to do is keep it that way and just say that I was sorry I wasn't able to protect him. That's basically all, that's about all I could say." She knew they would not have been able to have that conversation earlier, and we know that her progress in recovery was an important part of the change that made it possible.

Starr, MacLean, and Keating (1991) point out, in their review of the literature on generational effects of trauma, that sometimes parents who have been abused have blind spots that prevent them from adequately protecting their own children from abuse by others.

Ilona told us in the initial interviews that she had an image of the way she wished things had been when her children were young:

> In their younger years I would've liked to have been more stable, if you will, less abrasive, less caustic. That was part of my disease; that was part of the way that I was brought up, that I knew. And I didn't know better until I started thinking in terms of that there's got to be a better way. And I was the key, it was me. I had to change. And that's what I've worked on for the past seventeen or eighteen years, changing me, and that's what I work on now.

We have no doubt, both from what we learned about these women's stories and from work with clients who are survivors, that the more work women have done on their histories before they try to parent, the easier the process of parenting is likely to be. The implications of that are obvious, although usually not easy for therapists to implement. When working with late adolescents and young adults, therapists can help educate their clients to the knowledge that healthy parenting requires a degree of knowledge and acceptance of all parts of the self, and they are more likely to arrive at that when they have come to terms, to some degree, with their abusive histories. For survivors who already have children when they begin their healing, therapists can help frame these issues for them, guiding them to see why parenting is often so difficult for them and use their motivation to be good parents as a way to encourage them to hang tough through the difficult process of healing.

Our participants and their children will continue to experience and struggle with the residue from their abusive histories. It is impossible to avoid that. But therapists can help abuse survivors with children find ways to move beyond the dysfunctional legacies of their own histories and pass on their courage and resiliency. Survivors can also be helped to put these terrible stories into words so their children can gradually come to know and process this aspect of their legacy in ways that free the children from the burden of carrying their parents' emotions.

6

Relationships Outside the Family

Trauma survivors tend to get cut off from other people, partly because they have bad feelings about themselves and their families that lead to intense shame. Also they may want to hide the abuse to protect themselves or their families. Furthermore, some of their early experiences with relationships have been hurtful, leading them to mistrust connections. Despite this, even before treatment some survivors can have interpersonal connections. Some can even have good ones.

In this chapter we explore what our participants told us about their nonfamily relationships, that is, relationships with people, with pets, and sometimes with things. In the first section we present what we have learned about their relationships with people outside the family, first in childhood and then adulthood. (Therapy relationships are discussed in Chapter Seven.) Next we portray some of the struggles they told us about and the ways we believe these struggles and their efforts toward resolution reflect strength. Then we describe the importance to our participants of pets and occasionally dolls, particularly in childhood but sometimes in adulthood as well. The last section describes to whom and when they told their abuse stories and how this process reflected and further contributed to their resiliency. In each section we discuss the implications of our findings for therapists working with survivors.

A CARING ADULT OUTSIDE THE FAMILY

Both clinical lore and research literature suggest that a relation-ship with a caring adult outside the home can provide a life-saving source of support for children from dysfunctional families. Steven and Sybil Wolin (1993) describe resilient survivors as individuals who are particularly adept, even in childhood, at "recruiting" car-ing parent substitutes. We have seen the importance of such people as loving grandmothers or aunts and uncles in mediating the neg-ative effects of dysfunctional families. We wondered whether our participants had important childhood connections with adults and, if so, whether those connections were related to their resiliency.

Eight of our ten participants told us about an adult who cared about them, noticed their pain, and tried to intervene or somehow to buffer them from what was happening in their own families. Some of these people were members of their extended families, most notably grandmothers, who were able to convey their love and ap-preciation for them, even when they saw each other only occasion-ally. In addition three of the participants described nannies or baby-sitters from their earliest years who provided some support. Carrie remembered a baby-sitter she really liked who, she believed, was important to her. She said of this sitter and other adults: "I think that one of my strengths is I've somehow through my life kind of created, found people that I could connect with, or found people who cared about me, or just created families outside my family." We agree with Carrie that this has been one of her great strengths and believe that the loving connection she had with her mother during her first several years helped make her strong. Carrie had a template of what it felt like to be cared about and nurtured and therefore was able to seek nurturing from other adults when her mother was not available.

Therapists working with survivors can fruitfully explore with them whether there were such supportive individuals in their child-hoods, inside or outside the family. In their pain stemming from abuse, survivors sometimes forget the life-affirming relationships they had. If these existed, therapists can help by pointing out the importance of the fact that someone cared for them. Clients in the throes of remembering abuse often feel that they are and always have been totally unlovable and unworthy. A reminder that not everyone agreed with that assessment can be powerful and therapeutic.

As is common in the urban black community, Felicia had ties to people with titles like "Aunt" or "Grandma" who were not blood kin but who played an important role in her family life. Felicia felt close to a person she called Grandma who baby-sat with her while her mother worked. Felicia told us one story about Grandma standing up for her when her mother gave her a hard time. A teacher had said on her report card that Felicia was "really independent and sometimes too strong in the class in terms of [her] opinions and things." Felicia said, "And my Grandma looked at her and said, 'Well, she got all A's.'" That support meant a lot, but the connection did not prevent her Grandma's adult son and nephew from abusing Felicia. And Felicia said nothing about it.

Therapists working with African American clients in particular need to be mindful of the particular strengths of the extended family in fostering resiliency and may need to remind survivors of those strengths. Particularly because, as Wilson (1994) points out, there is so much shame about acknowledging sexual abuse outside the black community, white therapists need to be attuned to the positive aspects of some urban black families.

As we have described, teachers played a critical role in some participants' lives by recognizing their considerable abilities and by indicating that they valued these young people. For several, an important supporting role was played by camp and camp counselors. Other adults in the neighborhood sometimes reached out to these abused girls; for some, this care made a difference. Ilona was befriended by a maternal woman who lived in the same hotel she and her mother lived in. This woman often ate hotel meals with her, when she would otherwise have eaten alone, and she let Ilona know she cared for her. For a girl as neglected as Ilona, having an adult friend was important because it gave her a glimmer of an idea that she could be cared about and valued. A therapist for a survivor like Ilona should help her review her history for such positive connections and see the ways such ties reflected and enhanced her resiliency.

We see, from these and other stories, that the children with the least conflicted relationships with their primary caretakers, however dysfunctional, were most likely to be offered and to be able to receive help from others. Those with the least family support got the least help from others. As clients begin to develop a more differentiated and accurate view of themselves and their histories, it can help them understand the role their own early training in mistrust had in teaching them to hold all relationships at arm's length and to learn the ways they communicated that. The value in such work is that they can begin to view compassionately the young self they were, who could not allow helpful connections. This is better than seeing, as many do, their lack of early relationships as evidence of their unworthiness or hatefulness.

We see what these kinds of supports provided for our participants in childhood. Supports gave many a sense that they could be loved by someone and that someone believed they were of value. Teachers were in a unique position to communicate to these children that they were smart and could thus go far. Neighbors, "adopted" family members, and parents of friends provided other models for how people treat each other and for more normal, nurturant family life. Such modeling is central to resilient survivors' ability to imagine, and ultimately to work for, a different kind of life for themselves.

Interestingly, none of the participants described therapists as significant figures in their childhood. Although several had had contact with mental health professionals before college, none described the experience as especially important. However, therapists of abused children and adults need to understand their own potential role as one of these central people. Although the survivor is often one of many clients to the therapist, the therapist is often more central to the client, whether child or adult. The therapeutic relationship can be a major bridge to recovery, even though that relationship is subject to the same strains that survivors encounter in other close relationships. Second, the centrality of relationships to recovery should lead therapists to focus on and to encourage clients to develop and maintain close connections with others.

In our view, then, outsiders providing relationships, nurturance, and assistance to abused children can make an important difference. At least in this group of women, the outsiders did not provide the lifeline that the clinical literature has sometimes suggested for such connections, nor were they able to stop the abuse from happening. Nonetheless, the memory of good childhood connections can itself be a resource for adult survivors.

Mentors and Friends in Adulthood

We were primarily interested in the role of nonfamily adults in childhood in terms of their capacity to increase resiliency. Our interest in these relationships in adulthood had a somewhat different focus. Adult survivors of childhood sexual abuse often have difficulty with personal and social connections, as Cole and Putnam (1992) describe from a developmental perspective and Diane Elliot (1994) describes in her study of the relationships of professional women molested in childhood. Many have learned well to mistrust closeness. Further, we know from our clinical work that many resilient survivors contain and manage the intense and potentially problematic feelings that are the usual residue of their traumatic experiences by keeping some distance from people. Closeness often evokes these feelings. Thus we were interested to learn more about the adult relationships of our participants. We wondered if they had found people to support and mentor them and how they had fared with friendships.

Only two participants described mentors in adulthood, although we suspect their therapists sometimes played that role. Darlene had a greatly valued and supportive relationship with her academic adviser in her doctoral program. Galen described a supervisor and mentor at work when she was twenty-three. Unlike so many people in Galen's life, this supervisor was supportive of Galen and also respectful of her boundaries. Not only did she never approach Galen sexually but she said she would never do that—that it would never be appropriate, given their relationship. (Galen told us a number of stories that were painful to hear of people in positions of authority or mentorship, like the band director, who did violate her boundaries in one way or another.)

Carol Gilligan and her colleagues have emphasized the important role that making connections with others plays in normal female development (Gilligan, Lyons, & Hammer, 1990). From our interviews we learned that friendships with other women continued to play an important role in their lives. Friends provided support and often were the first people our participants told about the abuse. Participants also found in friendships the opportunity to experiment with ways of engaging in relationships that were often less threatening and more positive than those they had experienced in their families. Directly or indirectly, some of our participants told us that maintaining close and satisfying friendships was difficult.

Overall our participants described themselves as very satisfied with their circle of friendships. Beth could have been speaking for a number of them when she described how her friends "believe in me and are really good to me, keep me going." She talked about how she frequently reaches out to friends:

> I still just feel bad a lot and I'll call one of my friends. I'll often make three or four phone calls even during the day, because I kind of realize that my perceptions are skewed, particularly now that I'm dealing with the pain of the neighbor's abuse, and the depression. . . . Sometimes I need people, my friends bring me, almost like a reality check, bring me back into the world and not feel like

such a shit. Because some days I'm just in so much pain I just feel awful. So I'll talk to a friend and I'll realize I'm not so bad, I'm just feeling bad because I'm having these memories.

Beth has worked on her ability to reach out to friends, and we agree that it has been an important aspect of her recovery. She had come a long way from the isolated child she once was.

Ilona also described her friends as supportive and said, "There are some women friends that I have that are emotionally supportive. Then there's other women that I know they will turn to me in a crisis and in terms of if there is a crisis in my life I can turn to them." Particularly because Ilona did not have close peer relationships in childhood, we see her ability to establish reciprocal friendships in adulthood as a strong indicator of her resiliency and the growth she has experienced over time.

We are impressed with the extent to which a number of our participants did have strong and satisfying friendships, as well as the way their friendships improved as they moved forward in their recovery. Adult friendships are an important and relatively safe testing ground for new and healthier relationships in connection, as well as being intrinsically valuable. We encourage therapists to pay close attention to their clients' struggles with relationships, help them see and feel their own strength in their determination to have connections, and help them work through the issues that inevitably arise around interpersonal closeness. In our experience, it would be almost impossible to spend too much time in therapy on this fruitful area.

STRUGGLES WITH FRIENDSHIPS IN ADULTHOOD

Here we focus on our participants' adult friendships, most of which were and are positive relationships. However, most spoke about struggles within these relationships. We focus on those struggles here for two reasons: (1) we think the stories convey important information for therapists about what makes friendships difficult, and (2) they illustrate survivors' pride and satisfaction as they learned to sustain healthier connections, as well as their persistence in working to get to that place.

Felicia talked openly about her difficulties with friendships. She described herself as suspicious and as having difficulty with trust. She stated that she had many "one-sided friendships" with people who considered her a friend but whose feelings she did not reciprocate. In the initial interviews, she described herself as follows: "I have three layers around me, and the real Felicia is in here and most of my friends are out there [outer circle]. I never let people in that little circle. And the feelings sometimes get there, but I put a stop. And I keep them out because I know it could cause me trouble."

Felicia also spoke about how she liked being around people who "don't just talk" but who want to do things. She said, "You know how sometimes friends get together and they try to psychoanalyze you. I don't like that. Let's go to the theater; let's go do something. I don't want to hear all of your problems, and I don't want to tell you all of mine." Felicia seemed to feel drained by relationships and felt she had to protect herself from them. She did not seem to see other people as sources of support, although she was able to find some support in her relationship with her partner. Nonetheless, she continued to struggle to connect with others, despite how difficult and often unsatisfying it was to her. By the time of the follow-up interview six years later, she was much more comfortable in her friendships and had a number that she valued.

For a client like Felicia, these issues can provide fertile ground for important exploration in therapy. We would emphasize to her that although the story she tells about herself includes her view that others are not supportive, in fact she does continue to strive for connection, and that striving speaks louder than her words about her life-supporting longing and drive for connections.

In the initial interviews, when asked about what she would like her friendship circle to be, Helen said that she would choose to have a few close friends. "I have lots of friends now, but not intimate. I have a lot of friends there [in AA], a lot of people like me. But they don't know me." At that time, she told us she had a few close friends that she could be herself with, "but not fully. It would be nice if I could be myself." When we asked if she thought she might develop the kind of friendships she wanted, she said firmly, "Yup. Anything is possible. I'm determined. I want all the good stuff. I deserve it." She also described herself currently as being "right against the wall of fear. And it's scary and it's lonely. It's more lonely because I know it's there." As with Felicia, at the time of the follow-up interview she was much more comfortable with her friendships with women, felt they did know her, and felt significantly more able to trust. Unlike Felicia, Helen was more aware of her wish and need for connection and was determined to have intimate friendships. We are impressed with her courage in allowing herself to experience her loneliness. We would tell her that if she were our client.

Many other participants struggled with issues around intimacy, setting limits, and asking for help in relationships; some spoke about their tendency to isolate themselves and some about their need to reach out to others. Anne, whose mother knew no boundaries, talked about learning to set limits in her relationships with her friends: "I've discovered that a lot of my friends are co-dependent personalities. So I've had to get better at setting some limits, even in my friendships which in the past I would have just run from that person, or I would have felt uncomfortable." Anne connected her ability to set limits in her friendships with beginning to set limits with her mother before she died. She stated, "To be able to say to people it hurts me or it threatens me. Saying my feelings to someone in a friendship situation is sort of exhilarating."

For Janet as for Anne, this process of becoming more assertive with friends seemed to parallel confronting her family and setting limits with them. For both women, setting limits with friends was less frightening and better received than doing so with their families. Their friends responded positively and with understanding to the limit setting, which is partly a reflection of the type of people they chose for friends.

Asking for help was also challenging in participants' relationships with their friends; asking for help triggered uncomfortable feelings of shame and vulnerability. Our participants tended to avoid these feelings by being self-reliant and independent. Beth described this in the context of asking to stay with friends during an upcoming vacation: "I thought I was going to be able to stay with a friend, and it turns out I can't stay with her, so now I have to call someone else and see if I can stay with them. And I know if anybody calls me I'd be happy to have them stay with me and have a great time. But somehow for me to ask them triggers a lot of feelings of shame, that somehow I ought to be able to do this without asking for help." She was able to ask this of her friend; her discomfort did not stop her. We see this as part of her recovery and a reflection of her growing resiliency.

Difficulty asking for help also manifested itself in the way some participants, like Felicia, depended only on themselves. That asking for help and depending on others is hard for survivors is not surprising, considering that these women's independence and self-reliance enabled them to survive their histories.

Overall we see adult relationships with friends as complex and very important to our participants' recovery. On the side of their strength and resiliency was their continuing to reach out to others and their growing success in doing so; they continued to try to lessen their isolation and experience enjoyable and playful times. Another implicit aspect of their resiliency is that none described currently abusive friendships. Many were striving to learn to ask more of others and to maintain better boundaries in their friendships.

Even though these stories illustrate some of the struggles that women who have been abused in childhood face in developing friendships, they also show the strengths often seen in resilient survivors. Their most impressive strength is their determination to have good friendships and their willingness to work hard to develop them. Even before therapy, most had connections. Only a few of the women were really isolated before they began their recovery process, and by the time of the follow-up all of them had at least several comfortable and trusted friendships. Their stories illustrate what a strong resource friendships are for survivors.

RELATIONSHIPS WITH PETS AND THINGS

When we began thinking about this book, we had not planned to include a section on relationships with pets and inanimate objects. This section grew out of the passion with which our participants told us about their pets and cherished objects. It is not surprising that pets were important sources of comfort and support in childhood. Elena was eloquent when she talked about the importance of her two dogs. "I had two dogs in my life. When I was twelve we got another dog, and I realized later he was the singular stable love object in my house. He loved me no matter what. He slept beside my bed and all those things. And I realized that when he died, my sense of love in my parent's house died. He was really it."

In adulthood Elena recognized the depth of her connection to this dog and included him in a psychodrama: "I had my whole family lined up, telling me to stop talking about incest. And someone playing my dog, supporting me, right beside me, comforting me. I really did see that he was a source of comfort for me."

Unfortunately these tender and important connections with pets were often vulnerable to the vicissitudes of these families' lives. For example, in childhood Ilona was attached to a dog who was, she said, "very important to me; she loved me unconditionally, as I loved her unconditionally." But when Ilona was abruptly uprooted and sent to live in another city with strangers, as happened periodically, the dog was given away. She cried when she told us about it, and it was clear that she was still mourning. But it was also clear that her love for that dog was a reflection of her capacity to love, despite how little experience she had being loved. As her adult family and friendship ties illustrate, she continued to develop that ability.

Beth and Carrie both talked about the importance of their pets to their adult lives. Carrie told us, "My cat is really important to me. She's like my baby or something. I kind of like the fact that's she very much a people person herself, and she's not afraid of people. She likes to cuddle, and I figure that reflects a sense of safety, which I feel like I had had a role in creating, so I feel good about that."

A few of our participants told us about objects that had assumed importance to them in childhood. Galen gave us a wonderful example of her attachment to two dolls:

> I had this little doll called Clowny. I just feel like she's been through it all with me. I always feel really close to Clowny. And I also have this doll; her name's Joanne. I got her when I was about that high. And I chopped off all her hair when I was little because I thought it would grow back and it never grew back. But I put her at the top of the closet because I was mad. And then when I was coming out as a lesbian I brought her back down and dyked her all out. And then I would have her in my car, when I was eighteen, nineteen years old. And she would always be there with me in the car. She's sort of like my inner child.

Galen still had Clowny with her in her apartment. Darlene described the importance of a locket that her grandmother had given her: "One thing that's real important to me—the locket that my grandmother gave me. I'll wear it only on very special occasions because I don't want to lose it. But it's in my room where I can see it. And that means a lot to me. Once I thought I lost it, and I like ripped the house apart."

Darlene went on to say that it wasn't just the objects that were important to her but the meaning she attached to them and "the meaning other people placed on them when they gave them to [me]." We should note that many participants talked passionately about their relationships with books throughout their childhood and adulthood.

What seems important about our participants' relationships with pets and with objects is that these relationships provided some comfort during their childhood and sometimes into adulthood, when other people were often unreliable and even dangerous. Pets could provide and receive love and support. Unfortunately, pets were also vulnerable, and their loss could be devastating. Sometimes a thing, like a doll, could provide a sense of safety and nurturing. And books could open up the world of ideas and fantasy to a child. For childhood abuse survivors, their intense connections to pets or dolls were a reflection of their continued, life-saving ability to love. One role for therapists is to help their clients see this capacity and to appreciate it for the strength it is.

SHARING ABOUT ABUSE

A great deal of research has examined the importance of disclosing the feelings and thoughts generated by difficult life experiences and the impact of this disclosure on psychological and physical health (for example, Pennebaker, 1995 and 1997, and Harvey, Orbuch, Chwalisz, & Garwood, 1991). A number of researchers and clinicians have hypothesized that an important part of recovery from traumatic events is sharing the traumatic experiences. For these reasons, and the fact that many of our participants volunteered information about talking with friends, we were interested in what they had to say about sharing their abuse histories with others. Several women said they had first shared their abuse histories with peers or friends.

Darlene first disclosed her abuse history to a woman in college with whom she later became friends. This woman had come to her dorm to talk about date rape and had offered to talk with anyone who had been victimized. Darlene went to talk with her and ended up telling her about the abuse she had experienced, which she had not shared with anyone else. This woman became an advocate for Darlene throughout college, and they remained close friends. Darlene felt that reaching out to this woman was an early step in her recovery process—a step that fortunately was well received. This positive experience led her to reach out to others. Darlene said that in her current life, "I talk about [the abuse] essentially because I know a lot of women—I would say 80 percent of my women friends have been sexually abused or raped. We talk about our experiences together."

Anne had talked about some of the difficulties in her family with a childhood friend, and she continued to find sharing her experiences helpful in adulthood, telling us she was "processing some of it with friends of mine who are processing some of the same stuff, although not necessarily exactly the same." Anne was finding that her friends were understanding and comforted herself with this when she was upset. She told us that when she felt alone she would sometimes tell herself "X person would understand," and that made her feel better.

Beth described mixed experiences sharing her story of abuse and recovery with her friends. She said she made an effort to reach out to her friends when she needed support and stated, "There are a lot of people I can call up any time of the day or night and talk about what's going on with me." However, at times she felt her friends would get overwhelmed by what she told them and then could not listen. So in spite of her close friendships, Beth, like many other survivors, felt somewhat isolated when dealing with the abuse. At the time of the initial interviews, her solution was to start seeking out other women who had been through similar experiences, such as those in Incest Survivors Anonymous. By the follow-up interviews she had moved beyond her intense recovery process and was no longer particularly interested in discussing her history with anyone other than a therapist.

Like Beth and Darlene, many of our participants dealt with feelings of isolation engendered by their abuse histories by seeking out other women who had had similar experiences. Galen spoke about the importance of this for her recovery. She described how she started talking about her history when she first moved to a major city in the Northeast and began working at a women's residential treatment program. The staff was very aware of issues around trauma and abuse, and Galen began by disclosing her history to them. The support she received influenced her to return to that city after graduation because she felt she had a strong support network there. She also sought out women friends, particularly women in recovery who were "a bit older and sort of like big sisters or something." We see part of Galen's, Darlene's, and Beth's resilience reflected in their seeking out relationships with women who had had similar experiences, who could understand what they are going through, and who could validate their experience.

Carrie gave a particularly articulate description of the process at the follow-up:

> My pattern has been that I only share my abuse history with my close friends. I'm pretty careful who I tell, because I feel so vulnerable when I talk about it. I need to feel confident that the people I tell will be able to respond in a sensitive, caring way. I tend to worry about burdening people with the "heaviness" of my history. I also feel vulnerable telling people because of the stigma I feel in connection with being an incest survivor. On the other hand, I do have a number of close friends who I can and do talk with about my past, my feelings about the abuse, and how it affects me in the present.

As Carrie's comments suggest and as other participants told us, there were times in their lives when they reached out to people they thought were friends and attempted to share with them about their histories but then were not believed, were rejected, or were even blamed. In spite of these experiences, all of our participants were continuing to make friends and reach out to others; they continue to learn to take care of themselves in relationships so they can have the satisfying connections they want.

The stories from our participants about how they shared information about childhood sexual abuse with others helps illuminate what a complicated and important process sharing is. As the women told us, they needed to be able to tell some friends but found that telling did not always go so well, and even caring and well-meaning friends were not always able to hear such difficult information or to be sensitively responsive. Therapists need to appreciate both the importance of telling and the difficulty of finding the right way and the right person. Particularly if the therapist herself is not an abuse survivor, it is easy to underestimate the complexity of this task and thus be of less assistance to clients.

Part III

Processes and Strategies for Developing Resiliency

7

The Role of Psychotherapy

Psychotherapy is a central component of healing for most people with histories of childhood sexual abuse (see, for example, Courtois, 1988; Herman, 1992; van der Kolk, McFarlane, & Weisaeth, 1996). Our own experience as psychotherapists strongly supports that view. In this chapter we discuss what our participants told us about the role of therapy in their healing process. Their narratives have important implications for psychotherapists.

We had required as a selection criterion that all participants be in psychotherapy at the time of the interviews so they would have support for whatever might be stirred up by the research. But resilient trauma survivors usually get into therapy for their own reasons; collectively, our participants had had many years and many kinds of therapy.

These women had an average of nine years of individual therapy, some of it sporadic, some twice a month, but most often weekly and occasionally twice a week. In addition, several had been in group therapy (three in trauma groups, one in a more general group), one in couple's therapy, and one in adjunctive hypnotherapy; one had participated in psychodrama. Three of the women had been hospitalized at some point in their recovery. A majority were currently on medication. Six had attended one or more self-help groups such as Alcoholics Anonymous, Al-Anon, or Incest Survivors Anonymous, and several spoke of the value of self-help literature. Most of the women first began psychotherapy in their teens and twenties.

In this chapter we focus on what we learned from our participants within the context of each of the major forms of therapy— individual, group and family, hospitalization, and self-help.

INDIVIDUAL PSYCHOTHERAPY

For virtually all participants, individual psychotherapy was a central component of their recovery, often *the* central component. Many expressed deep appreciation for that avenue of healing. Our participants described two major ways that therapy contributed to their recovery. First, they highly valued having a person and context they could begin to trust, sometimes for the first time in their lives. Second, during their therapy they could begin to cognitively reframe their experiences. Specifically, therapy helped them understand what had happened to them in childhood, taught them how to tolerate and deal with strong emotions, provided support and reassurance, and coached them on dealing with current relationships. At least one talked about therapy, particularly hypnotherapy, as a way to recover memories.

Finding a Therapist

At the time of the interviews all participants had therapists they appreciated and trusted. Some had been fortunate in finding a good therapist they could work with from the beginning and had continued with that individual over a period of years. Others had gone through a number of therapy experiences before finding one that worked for them. Janet had had several unhelpful experiences before finding a therapist she liked. She described the first person she saw in college, when she went to the counseling center: "He sat behind his desk. He had the tape recorder on, and he was like, 'Um hum.' It was a shame, because I was reaching out, and if I had had a good therapist at that point I would have been able to do some work. It was just awful. He made me feel like I was crazy, and I said, 'I can't talk to this guy.' So I didn't get the help that I needed."

Partly as a consequence of this failed attempt, Janet did not get therapy until after her experience with EST evoked memories of abuse. She tried to go to the EST therapists but said, "They were very unhelpful, because they would tell me to get off it, and I knew that wasn't right." This shows how uninformed members of the mental health community can interfere with individuals' recovery. It also illustrates Janet's remarkable clarity about what she needed and her willingness to persist until she found that. We believe therapists should take seriously their clients' perceptions of what they need in therapy. They often have genuine wisdom about themselves, even when they can't articulate why they need a particular kind of therapist or a particular approach.

Darlene had an especially difficult path before she found a therapy she felt good about. She had been in outpatient psychotherapy with a therapist who had convinced her that because of her strong suicidal feelings it would be safer to do some of the recovery work in a hospital. During that two-month hospitalization, Darlene said she "was not exactly cooperating. So my outpatient therapist then decided, because I wasn't cooperating she wasn't going to see me when I got out. But she decided not to tell me that; she had the hospital staff tell me. And then she wouldn't return any of my phone calls, which set me off even more. I was pissed and then I became like every person's nightmare. I was furious."

In the follow-up interview Darlene added an important point. She had not been comfortable telling us in the initial interviews that she had always felt her therapy was compromised by her level of intellect. Referring to earlier therapists, she said, "I somehow felt that they were not quite sharp enough or witty enough to work fully with me or adequately with me and understand the depth of my experience." When she relocated for her internship, she found an African American therapist who she felt was an intellectual match for her. Darlene said this new therapist was "the first of any of my therapists to set limits on any behavior—verbal or physical—and who challenged me, who questioned me, and really made me work." Darlene said she had always represented her history through drawings and poetry. No previous therapist had ever explored them or asked her about her feelings about any of it, whereas her new therapist pushed for answers, came back to things to explore them in more depth. Darlene continued:

> She also challenged me cognitively in terms of discussing my abuse and extended the therapy to cover a whole range of issues, including what it means to be an African American woman. I felt that her willingness to initiate discussion about many topics in many ways gave me permission to address these issues. And I did not feel I was betraying my family or the black community by disclosing secrets to someone who was outside of the race. I think those allowed me a greater freedom to really utilize the psychotherapy process.

Part of Darlene's difficulty settling into a productive therapy was the fact that her earlier therapists were white. Although some therapists and clients work comfortably across racial boundaries, it can be more difficult to establish trust, and trust is particularly problematic for abuse survivors. We agree with Darlene that it is the therapist's responsibility to initiate discussions of this complex issue early in treatment. Some individuals give up after one or several unsatisfactory efforts at therapy. As was true with Janet, Darlene's resilience was expressed in her persistence in finding an appropriate therapist.

Felicia could not afford private therapy and had managed to make the state system work well for her, even though she had had to change therapists periodically. She described dissatisfaction with her first therapy: "I stopped because I'm a goal-oriented person; I would like to work on this and this and this. And it didn't seem that

I was getting out of it what I needed." At this point her therapist—
a psychiatric resident—relocated, and Felicia stopped therapy. She
also stopped taking medication because she didn't feel it was regu-
lated properly. She tried but was unsuccessful in getting her care-
givers to listen to her concerns. In Felicia's view, the short-term
consequence of stopping treatment was that she became more symptomatic and ended up hospitalized. However, her resilience was reflected in the integrity of her commitment to staying away from a
therapy that did not feel right for her and finally finding therapies
that worked.

One essential lesson for therapists is to take seriously what abuse
survivors say about what they believe they need in therapy. Although clients are not always completely right, their intuitions are
often very instructive for therapists. In the case of minority clients,
taking clients' wishes seriously may mean committing oneself to
becoming more culturally competent or to facilitating a transfer to
a colleague who is. Therapists need to be aware of which clients
they work best with and which they need to refer.

Learning to Trust

Many of our participants were deeply appreciative of the fact that
they had come to trust their therapists and that their therapist honored that trust. Ilona was asked to whom she had told parts of her
story. She said she had talked to her therapist, Elizabeth: "I'm sure
that I've talked with Elizabeth. She was the one that I really was able
to communicate, connect to. There was this empathy between us."

Felicia talked of one of her therapists: "But I did begin to trust
her, I opened, I really got to the issues. And she said I could say
what I needed to say, and I don't have to take care of her; I don't
have to worry about what I might say and how it affects her." Later
she said, with great clarity:

I know that I can in therapy now be safe and not be hurt.
But, however, if I think there's a red flag, I'll say, "Can

you explain what you mean by that?" Or "I don't agree with that." Or like for instance I know you can't trust everyone and that people are human and they are going to make mistakes. And I know that therapists aren't exempt from that. So if I see anything that I don't really like, I will say to them, "Wait a minute, I want to understand this. What are you saying?"

We hope that all therapists can appreciate the strength in Felicia's ability to say, "Wait a minute. What are you saying?" even though it might feel like a challenge to the therapist's authority. Such comments often reflect survivors' significant progress acknowledging feelings and needs, and asserting them in the therapeutic context.

Part of the safety of the context is knowing that therapists usually won't raise issues with clients until the clients are ready to deal with them. Anne gave a nice example of how pacing contributed to her trust in her therapist. The interviewer had asked Anne how long ago her therapist had first said to her that what had happened in her family was abuse. She replied, "It might have been maybe six years ago. It wasn't from the beginning. I thought that he was really clear and very direct, but I think he's also very gentle and doesn't say things until people are ready to hear them. And he said that about the abuse too. He said that sometimes people aren't ready to hear things."

Here the issue of pacing is crucial. Traumatic experiences get frozen in people's minds because the associated ideas and emotions are simply intolerable. Good therapy must gradually increase clients' tolerance for such ideas and emotions and not force them to confront the reality of their histories until they have the inner strength to experience the feelings without becoming overwhelmingly frightened of them or disorganized.

Even when our participants believed their therapy was safe, not all of them were yet able to trust. When we first met Helen, she had been working with her therapist for three years. We asked if she felt she could be fully open with her therapist. She said, "No. Too scary. I would like that to happen but no way, not yet. She's trying to get me to break that wall to allow her to be important, but I think I've only cried in there once. Too close. The fear is like a wall."

Establishing a relationship of trust is probably the single most important task for the therapist of a trauma survivor. Given that survivors' trust has been badly and often repeatedly violated so early in life, this is not easy; it can require years of therapy. Establishing trust includes creating a context in which clients can speak up for themselves, as Felicia had, and pacing the work so that clients are not retraumatized by exposure to intense negative emotions before they are ready to deal with them.

Framing and Reframing

A major part of the therapeutic work these women did was to get help understanding what had happened to them and seeing how the experiences had affected them. Sometimes this involved integrating formerly disparate pieces of their memories or life experiences into a coherent whole. Often trauma survivors come to therapy with distorted views of themselves and others. Much of the work of therapy is revisiting and revising these views. Anne spoke for all participants when she told us, "Certainly my therapist has had a big influence on different ways of looking at things and different ways of thinking about things." Felicia told us that she had just discovered, through therapy, that she only felt that she was worth something if she was helping someone else.

Elena talked of seeing a therapist briefly who listened to her story and "came back to me with a continuum [a time line] of my life. It was the first time I had ever viewed my life as anything other than discrete and unrelated events. And it was a new concept to me, that she was able to show me that it was my life, continuous, across those years. And that there were connections that could be drawn between those years."

Beth described her disappointment when her father responded badly to her invitation to attend a family therapy session with and for her, saying he wouldn't go if his ex-wife was going to be there.

> I said, "Well Dad, this meeting is for me. It's not about Mom." And he starting saying that my mother was trying to manipulate his life. And that's real sad. And, as one of my therapists pointed out, that it was clear from his reaction that that's probably what happened when I was a kid, which is why I didn't bring my needs up. Because any time I brought my needs up, a conflict between my parents became the focus, and not whatever need that I had. So I learned not to talk about what I needed.

Our participants also told us that their therapist helped reframe previous views of what had happened. Helen was telling the psychiatrist at the hospital about an experience from her childhood, "and the woman shrink that I was with that day said, 'My God, that's traumatic!' And all of a sudden for a minute it was like, 'Yeah, it is.' And then I said, 'No, it wasn't; it's not.' For one minute I thought it was traumatic. If I could picture another little girl seeing her mother's teeth punched out at such a young age, that's traumatic. But then I went to my survivor mode and just said, 'No, it was no big deal.'" Even though Helen could not then hold the awareness that these events had been traumatic, she heard it from the psychiatrist and over time was able to change her own understanding of her experience.

In another example of reframing, Anne told of describing to her therapist what it was like when her husband made love to her. "And my therapist said, 'Well, that's molestation, that's not sex.' I mean there were no hugs or anything afterward. There was no tenderness, and no kindness, and no real caring."

In an amusing exchange about reframing, Anne described a conversation with her therapist about trust: "And I said, 'I don't have a problem with trust. I trust everyone.' He said, 'That's a problem with trust!'" They went on to explore the ways she had been too trusting or too open with people. She said, "I have become more wary, more careful."

Anne gave a particularly nice example of the cognitive shift experienced by one of the participants as she learned to take more responsibility for her own behavior and understand how it contributed to the difficulties in her life:

> I think I got really serious about my own personal therapy, because a lot of it was marital therapy for a good long time. And when I began to see part of the problems in the marriage had to do with my childhood and were really my issues. . . . It was so easy to blame my husband for everything. Because he's just sometimes so right out there. And my participation in the difficulties was more subtle. I began to see my responsibility. And that of course is an enormous leap when you begin to realize it is not everyone else's fault at all. And that's a freeing thing, too. Because if it isn't everyone else's fault and you're responsible for some of it, then you can also do something about it. If it's always someone else's fault, then gee, there's really no hope; there's really not much you can do about it.

Cognitive reframing—helping clients revise their stories to better fit with the reality of their histories and their adult lives—is a major component of trauma therapy. Dysfunctional families often insist that their abused children view the family and themselves in a totally skewed way. For example, the abused child may be seen as causing problems because she is evil, or a parent may say he is doing

his daughter a favor by introducing her to sex. These strongly in-
duced stories that distort reality are deeply confusing to survivors
because they conflict so deeply with their own inner experiences.
Therapists need to spend a great deal of time helping clients clarify
what did happen and how they experienced it. As several participants exemplified, therapeutic conversations about these issues
often need to be repeated many times before clients can begin to
make use of them in their lives.

Dealing with Strong Emotions

Learning to tolerate and make use of strong negative emotion is a
key component of trauma therapy (Linehan, 1993; Olio & Cornell, 1993). Our participants gave many examples of how their
therapists helped them develop the inner resources to "sit with"
the powerful emotions caused initially by abuse and then evoked
whenever they were triggered into reexperiencing them. Felicia described her continued reactivity when things reminded her of the
abuse or her abuser. But she added, "I'm learning how to deal with
it in therapy now, and sometimes I'll see someone that might look
like him, but I don't have that same fear." Later in the interview,
Felicia said she had learned in therapy that one of her therapists
had told her she tends to intellectualize things. "So I'm trying to
learn how to; I'm still a baby when it comes to emotional things
and how to handle it." The interviewer said to Beth it sounded as
if nobody had given her the space to be sad about all the losses in
her life. She replied, "Well, that's what I'm working on in my therapy, but I'm so overwhelmed with a lot of stuff [feelings], it just
takes a long time."

Therapy also played a crucial role in helping our participants
recognize and deal with their rage; several struggled with rage
throughout their recovery. Through therapy they came to see the
connection between the rage and their histories. We have described
Darlene's rage when her outpatient therapist refused to see her after
her hospitalization and then refused to take her phone calls.

Darlene was assigned an outpatient therapist by the hospital and met with that woman, but she was still furious and, in her own view, very difficult. What seemed to Darlene to turn things around was her therapist's ability to tolerate her anger.

> I think that in that year I did a lot of testing as to whether she was going to take off when the going got a little rough or unpleasant. And I think she took a hell of a lot of abuse. She got it personally, even for stuff she didn't deserve, it was just like it all went to her, and she became the total asshole of the world and probably got a lot of stuff from the previous therapist who walked. And then I think I must've figured out that she wasn't going any place or wasn't going to take off. Then I started talking to her about little stuff, and then it worked out.

Although Darlene emphasizes how hard that process was on her therapist, it was also hard on Darlene. As we have mentioned before, the fact that she is African American and her therapists were Caucasian could not have made the process any easier.

According to Darlene's description, she sorely tested her therapist before she felt ready to settle down and work in therapy. Often clients do test their therapist's ability to deal with their strong feelings by expressing unfair anger, disappointment, or rage at the therapist. Therapists who want to work with trauma survivors need to have the inner and outer resources to deal with strong feelings themselves before undertaking this work. (McCann and Pearlman [1990] have written persuasively about the emotional difficulties that the practice of trauma therapy can create for therapists.) Therapists' inner resources often relate to their own therapeutic work around childhood griefs, whether traumatic or not, and to the amount of time and skill they devote to self-care. Outer resources include some kind of ongoing supervision-consultation context in which to talk over the work and what it feels like to be the target of such intense emotions.

Getting Support and Reassurance

Most of our participants spoke of times when they looked to their therapist for support and reassurance. Helen said that when she first remembered the cult abuse, she just cried and cried. She said, "And I called my therapist, and I just tried to reassure myself that I'm still a good person."

Like the other participants, she tried hard not to burden her therapist with phone calls. "I want to call my therapist. I really love her a lot. But the thing, she says I can call her sometimes, she said, within reason, like not too late at night or something unless it was a major thing. But then I'd be calling her all the time, so I try not to call her, because I just want to save it [for when it was] a real urgent thing. So I sometimes don't call her when I really want to call her during the week. I try not to."

Here Helen describes her efforts to protect her therapist and protect the relationship at the same time she was trying to cope with the extremely painful process of trauma therapy. We have seen this protectiveness often in our research participants and in our clients. Helen's therapist made herself accessible for phone calls, even when there was no extreme emergency, but also suggested boundaries such as that Helen not call late at night. There is disagreement among therapists of survivors about how much phone or other access to the therapist outside of regularly scheduled sessions is most helpful. Our participants suggested (and we have found in our own therapies with survivors) that it helps the therapy if it is possible to allow some flexibility around phone contact and other related issues. Ultimately, though, the decision has to rest on the personal comfort, preference, and style of the therapist.

Beth emphasized a different way her therapist provided support and reassurance. She felt discouraged about being so preoccupied with the sexual abuse she had suffered. She told us that sometimes her friends could not really be helpful because "they're just not trained for it. But my therapist told me it will get easier because it won't be so much front and center." She was learning not to always blame herself when things went wrong around her. "But I get tired and sometimes I still feel bad about myself. But now it doesn't last so long, and I can, worse comes to worse, I'll go see my therapist in a couple of days and say something, and he or she will say, 'Well, gee, but look at all this other stuff you've got.'"

The work of recovering from traumatic abuse is exceedingly painful. To be able to tolerate the distress, clients need support and reassurance from their therapists. Therefore, therapists who are not abuse survivors may need to be alert to the possibility of underestimating the psychological pain their clients are enduring and the amount of support they require.

Getting Coaching and Advice

Some participants described instances in which their therapists had helped them figure out what to do with regard to some issue. Ilona called her therapist when she was in a quandary about whether to participate in this research project. Her therapist suggested that Ilona consider whether she really wanted to do this and that if Ilona thought it might be too triggering, she might think of some other way to contribute to the project. In another example, Beth's therapist had encouraged her to find ways to be peaceful, including eliminating caffeine from her life because her life had been so agitated and she had been so jittery. Also Beth said that one of her therapists recommended she tell her son that she had been abused as a child, probably so he could better understand his mother's depression. (This last is consistent with Dan Bar-On's [1995] understanding of ways to reduce the intergenerational transmission of trauma).

Anne gave many examples of this kind of assistance from her therapist. When her husband was outrageously offended by what he considered her inappropriately seductive clothes, she said, "My therapist says that it doesn't match up with anything to do with the way

I dress. But it's how he perceives it, and if I don't want to precipitate this kind of response in him, then I shouldn't wear those things." Anne reaffirmed how helpful this kind of coaching had been for her. "And a lot of times when I'm getting in hot water I say to myself, what would [my therapist] say? What should I do here? How would he? So in those times when I'm not seeing him every week, that carries me through, too."

In a striking example of the helpfulness of a therapist's coaching, Anne saw her sister's therapist in Florida four times before confronting their mother about her current emotionally abusive behavior. She described this exchange: Anne said, "I can't do this, I can't do this, yes, I can, yes I can." The therapist said, "Keep telling her how you feel, keep telling her how you feel, and she's going to come around to telling you how she feels."

Coaching clients with histories of abuse about how to respond in problematic situations is one important function for therapists. Often included are ways to avoid triggering situations or ways to represent the client's feelings and needs in interpersonal contexts. Over time, clients can begin to anticipate their therapists' suggestions when they are in such situations and eventually to internalize these ideas in their own repertoire of responses.

Recovering Memories

Several participants talked about the use of psychotherapy as a way to recover memories of abuse; two had been sent by their therapists to hypnotherapists for that purpose. They had had some memories, but their therapists thought there might well be others. Beth found the hypnotherapy experience powerful and convincing. "Since last May I've been in hypnosis with a female therapist who specializes in sexual abuse in order to pull up memories of sexual abuse that my regular therapist suspected were there and, in fact, now we know were there."

Although Beth had remembered incidents of abuse by her mother and father, she said she had not remembered a series of molestations by an adolescent male neighbor when she was about five. She added:

> It's funny, because I don't know how much you know about hypnosis, but there's the rational, kind of businesswoman, number-cruncher part of me that says, "Nah! That stuff never happens." But fortunately in every trance I'd come up with a memory of something I'd never never remembered, and then with it would be something I did remember. In one case, while I was being molested I was being held down by my ankles. It was really painful in the trance, and when I woke up, I couldn't walk on my ankles because they hurt so much. And I remember telling my mother, at about this time [in childhood], that my ankles hurt. And I had a hard time walking home from the session. That, to me, is proof that it happened.

As an aside, we have some concerns about the reliability of memories recovered through the use of hypnosis. This subject is extremely controversial in the field and in the culture just now.[1] However, in this instance Beth told us that her memory of this neighbor and the molestation were validated by statements made by her mother and a sister.

As a number of researchers have reported (reviewed by Martha Rogers, 1995), the majority of trauma survivors have continuous memory of all or part of their abuse. Some, especially those abused at a younger age or for longer periods, can lose all of their conscious memory of the events until these are triggered by some later experience. Many who do not remember fully what happened to them but know that something happened come to therapy asking their therapists to help them recover those memories. Often they want the full memories back quickly so they can get on with their lives. However, a strong emphasis on memory recovery is unlikely to be useful to survivors of incestuous childhood abuse. Their therapists' more important task is to strengthen clients' capacity to tolerate unpleasant emotions and then to learn all of the ways their difficult history has colored and limited their adult lives. This is not to say that therapists should shy away from helping their clients explore what they know about their histories, nor should therapists refrain from helping them expand that awareness as clients begin to see things in a different perspective and to remember things they had not before. But recovery of memory should not be a central focus. When therapists do undertake memory recovery with clients, they should do so carefully to avoid shaping or influencing clients' views. At the same time, the therapist should not be so cautious and distant that she cannot provide reasonable support for the client in this difficult part of the work.

GROUP AND FAMILY THERAPY

Seven of our ten participants had been in some formal group therapy setting, and one was in periodic couple's therapy. Two others were actively considering a group experience but had not begun. Four had participated in trauma groups; two followed the short-term model described by Judith Herman (1992); one (Helen) joined an ongoing dissociative identity disorder (formerly multiple personality disorder) cult survivor group; and one attended a support group for trauma survivors offered by a college counseling service for students. Two were currently in general, mixed-gender psychotherapy groups. Elena had attended an Ellen Bass workshop and also had participated in a number of psychodrama groups. Many years before the interview, Janet had been in EST and had begun to recover memories through that experience. Four had met with one or more family members, in the presence of a therapist, to process issues related to their histories.

With the exception of Janet's EST experience, the women were very positive about their group experiences. Beth, who had been in a general group for seven years, said she felt it was in the group that she "really learned how to connect with people, because I didn't know how to connect with people. And I've learned healthy connections, connections where you can talk about issues and talk about problems and not feel like you're being destroyed if you're in a relationship."

She said she learned things about herself in group as well. For example, she told us she always asked lots of questions, even when she was new in the group. "I finally figured out when I was in group therapy that I would ask questions because my mother would then get mad at me for asking so many questions, and that's the way I would get attention. I mean, it was negative attention, but that was the only attention I got."

Carrie felt very supported by her group, which she joined when she found herself struggling with issues of commitment in an intimate relationship. Her first memory of abuse was triggered by a group discussion about her relationship with her father. At the time of the initial interviews, she had been in the group for almost four years.

Elena had participated in a weekend workshop run by Ellen Bass in Santa Cruz. "A phenomenal thing. And I would advise anyone beginning to deal with it or in any stage to get in a group. When I started doing my therapy and my therapist said she didn't want me in a group, she thought it would dissipate what I was doing. She didn't know. She's never worked with a survivor before, and she was wrong."

We agree with Elena as well as experts in the field such as Judith Herman (1992) that groups are often a crucial aspect of the recovery of trauma survivors. Because so much of the destructive aftereffects of childhood abuse are expressed in difficult interpersonal relationships in adulthood, well-run groups often provide an ideal context for seeing the problem *in situ*, having an opportunity to explore it then and there, and finding other ways of responding. Groups tend to generate intense emotions; they can be dangerous for survivors when the group therapist does not know how to work constructively with that intensity. But a well-run group, as one part of the treatment for childhood sexual abuse, is often of crucial importance.

Elena also had several experiences of psychodrama in weekend groups led by her individual therapist, and she described how powerful and effective they were. She talked of her astonishment when such an experience showed her that it was possible to change an inner script she carried around about her experiences:

> I remember learning that I could for myself change the outcome, through psychodrama, decide it could end differently, recreate the scenario, whatever it was, but then decide to end it very differently. And the first time [my therapist] told me that, my eyes got wide and my mouth fell open and I said, "What! What do you mean I can change the ending!? That's not how it was!" And it was just such a hard concept for me to get; it just blew me away. It was very effective, but it just never occurred to me.

When prompted for more details, she described a psychodrama in which the person playing her child self was able to stop the abuser by pushing him off. "It gave me another sense of control, of taking back my life, to be able to change the ending." (The literature on the use of psychodrama in therapy with abuse survivors is relatively recent, so we are not sure how to respond to Elena's experiences of rewriting the past, in a manner of speaking [Hudgins, in press; Hudgins & Toscani, 1998].)

Ilona and Janet had each done twelve-week structured trauma groups on the Herman model and found them helpful. Janet said, "It was great. It was really very hard to do; I was very symptomatic during it, throughout the group, but it was very good. I definitely broke through in ways in that group."

All of the participants who had met with a therapist and one or more family members to process something about their history or current relationships found it an important and valuable experience. Beth met with her mother and her mother's therapist, at her mother's invitation, to talk with her for the first time about the abuse. Her mother was able to confirm some of Beth's experiences with corroborating information, which was important to her.

Our participants reinforced what we, as trauma therapists, already knew—that groups can be important sources of support and healing for survivors in recovery. These women made use of many different types of groups, almost all of which were helpful in validating their experiences and helping them heal. The main caution we took from our participants' discussion of group treatments is that it can be triggering if exposure to traumatic material is not managed well by the group therapists. Therapists referring clients to group treatment need to ensure that the therapists involved are knowledgeable and experienced in the management of traumatic material in a group setting.

HOSPITALIZATION

Three of our participants had been hospitalized in the course of their recovery. Darlene had become depressed and suicidal during her therapy and once thought she had lost control and hit her partner, although she had not. Shortly after, she agreed to a voluntary hospitalization suggested by her psychotherapist (as we described earlier in the chapter). She was in the hospital for about two months; most of her stay was difficult, and Darlene was resistant and angry. During this time, her outpatient therapist decided to discontinue Darlene's treatment when she was discharged and communicated only with the hospital staff, asking them to tell Darlene. She also refused to respond to Darlene's many efforts to reach her by phone. Darlene was furious, and at the time of the initial interviews still felt it was inappropriate and unethical behavior. In retrospect, she was not sure that her hospitalization had been helpful.

Unlike Darlene, Felicia had better outcomes from her hospitalizations. As we have described before, she was very stressed from having to deal with an abuse case in her job as a security officer. Her legs became increasingly paralyzed, and her physicians wanted her to have a complete neurological workup; they recommended hospitalization. Over the course of a summer of hospitalization, they eventually were able to diagnose her as having a conversion disorder and put her on medication. They told her she needed to change jobs to reduce stress but, as she explained to us, she was in denial and went right back to her stressful job. Shortly afterward she was admitted to a hospital that had a trauma unit. During the course of that brief inpatient stay, the staff convinced her that she needed to do what the doctors said, which was to go into outpatient psychotherapy, follow her medication regime, and go on disability insurance. She did so, and the second hospitalization was a major turning point in her commitment to recovery.

Similarly, Helen was helped by hospitalizations. She had gone to Al-Anon to deal with her mother's alcoholism after her mother's death. In Al-Anon, she realized that she herself was alcoholic and began to try to stop drinking. She said of that time in her life, "I felt like I was going to die. I was in the pits of hell. I just needed a spiritual uplifting, and that's something I needed more. I wasn't getting it. Also the memories starting coming up, four and a half months sober." After four months of struggling with sobriety, she wanted more help and called a detoxification center to inquire about programs. "[The woman who responded to phone calls] must've seen through my denial because she said, 'Oh yeah, we have a two-week program. Sure you can concentrate on the Al-Anon part of it.' And once I got there, I found out there isn't a two-week program, and they don't focus on Al-Anon." After ten months of sobriety, Helen chose to spend a month in a hospital that had a specific trauma program. At the follow-up interview, she told of a third brief voluntary hospitalization. In her view, all of these experiences were very helpful.

From these three participants' experiences, it seems that hospitalization can be a helpful option for clients who are suicidal or need help dealing with substance abuse if the hospitalization is handled well by the treating therapist. Clearly, the best situation occurs when the client decides she needs to be hospitalized. Therapists should be aware that involuntary hospitalization can disempower and retraumatize clients. In dealing with an outpatient client who has to be hospitalized, the therapist must understand that hospitalization can be experienced as abandonment. When clients are hospitalized, the outpatient therapist should work closely with the inpatient team and maintain contact through the hospital stay. Darlene's very difficult and destructive experience of abandonment by her therapist while she was hospitalized provides a cautionary tale: therapists treating trauma survivors must get the support they need themselves so that they do not become so overwhelmed by their clients that they abandon them.

Furthermore, hospital settings that are not sophisticated in treating trauma survivors are not likely to respond helpfully or to have inpatient programs that facilitate a survivor's recovery. Units with well-trained, knowledgeable staff can provide an important part of the treatment for some survivors.

SELF-HELP

In the interviews we asked about participants' experiences with any aspect of the self-help movement. Four had been to one of the incest survivors' organizations (Survivors of Incest Anonymous or Incest Survivors Anonymous); four had made some use of Alcoholics Anonymous or its spinoffs (Al-Anon, Adult Children of Alcoholics); and several others had been in similar, leaderless groups. A number mentioned reading the self-help literature.

Their experiences with the self-help groups were mixed, although more positive than negative. Beth said of an incest survivors' group meeting, "The good thing is I feel kind of like I belong places now, where I used to I felt my whole life like I didn't belong anywhere. And one of the places I belong is the Incest Survivors group. That helps a lot." Darlene's experience was very different. "I went a few times with one of my friends who used to go but it was more overwhelming than anything else. . . . At that point in my life, because it was an unstructured group, I often just came away feeling more overwhelmed. I heard all this stuff and there really wasn't any processing of that. It left me feeling kind of fragmented after the group. It just wasn't the kind of group for me."

In contrast, she talked of going with a friend to Narcotics Anonymous meetings. "I found those more helpful for me, because a lot of people talked, like the family dysfunction stuff I think it, there's a lot of overlap whether it's children of alcoholics or child survivors of sexual abuse."

Helen did not find the incest survivors' leaderless groups helpful but did benefit from AA. She found that AA helped her maintain her sobriety and see herself and her behavior more clearly. She commented, "It's funny, when I first came into AA, I heard this woman from the podium say, 'You don't have to get laid for a hug.' And that has stuck with me, and that's what I want. I want to have the hugs; I don't want to get laid, and sometimes I want to get laid because that's the only way I know. But I hate it."

Ilona had had an important experience over a number of years at Overeaters Anonymous and learned a different way of thinking about herself and her difficulties. In her early period with that group, she lost a lot of weight, and as she learned the way she used food to silence her feelings, she started to have her feelings, which then allowed her to begin to work on her history of extreme trauma and neglect.

As for reading the self-help literature, Carrie found it useful. "Sometimes when I make love I just have to stop in the middle and

I can't continue, and couple of the books say, 'Hey, don't worry about it; you're taking care of yourself by doing that because somehow your body can't take the intensity of the feelings right then.' And that was really reassuring because now I saw, well, that's a consequence of the abuse, and it's not something inherent to me and it'll get better."

Carrie's comment reflects what a number of our participants might say: "Indirectly I think that the whole self-help recovery movement has made an impact on my life in a positive way. . . . There is something about the whole recovery movement that I think is really empowering."

Our participants had found that attending self-help groups and reading self-help literature were largely positive experiences. Groups such as Incest Survivors Anonymous tended to be less helpful when they offered unmediated exposure to traumatic material. Although the lack of hierarchy and designated leadership in these groups is one reason many survivors find them so empowering, these same characteristics can result in survivors being overwhelmed by others' traumatic stories. Therapists must be wary of such groups' potential for triggering should their clients attend or consider attending them. Because these meetings lack professional leadership, without even the degree of structure offered by AA groups, trauma clients' distress may not be addressed or attended to in the meeting. Therapists may want to work with clients on a plan for how to handle it if they become triggered during a meeting. Sometimes clients should be encouraged to participate in less trauma-focused self-help groups such as AA or in groups led by trained professionals. The self-help literature can also be an important supplement to other kinds of recovery work. Many therapists suggest particular books or newsletters to their clients. When therapists invite clients to bring their reactions to these readings back into therapy for discussion, the results can be particularly useful.

Although all of our participants were significant consumers of formal and informal mental health services, and all highly valued the help they had gotten through these methods, they also knew that there is life outside of therapy. Galen put it well: "I don't like to just inundate myself, therapize my whole being, be a workaholic about my healing process. Because I feel like I've done a lot of work and it's paying off and I just want to enjoy it."

Note

1. As psychologist Daniel Brown and his colleagues have suggested (Brown, Sheflin, & Hammond, 1996), hypnosis is not currently considered the safest way to recover memories because people in a hypnotic state appear to be so susceptible to influence. Furthermore, the courts are wary about the accuracy of memories recovered in trance states.

8

The Management of Feelings

Emotions constitute a major part of people's experience, and since the beginning of psychology as a field, we in the profession have tried to understand emotions. Mental health treatment is often focused on emotional well-being. Trauma creates such intense and distressing feelings that victims' abilities to cope with them are overwhelmed. In fact, mental health researchers (for example, van der Kolk and Fisler [1994]; Olio and Cornell [1993]) have suggested that many of the symptoms of trauma can be seen as consequences of the enormity of feelings. Therefore, the way people handle their traumatic emotions is of great importance to resiliency.

Overall, our participants varied on a number of important dimensions of feelings, including their predominant type of feeling, the range of feelings they expressed, and the complexity of their feelings. Some participants were mostly angry; others expressed more sadness. A significant number also reported feeling hopeful. Some expressed just a few feelings, others many.

Our participants talked about important feelings involving such areas as their history of abuse, their recovery process, and the many kinds of relationships they had experienced, as well as school and work. Here we present an overview of the feelings that were manifest in many different contexts and relationships. We focus on the variety of ways our participants coped with their emotions and suggest implications for therapists. We, like others in the field, consider the management of feelings to be one key to resiliency, along with self-care and meaning making. We were intrigued by the women's descriptions of their childhood and adult strategies for managing feelings because we saw that childhood strategies often predicted the adult style of management. Not surprisingly, as adults they had a greater range of strategies available to them.

In this chapter we first describe the strategies our participants told us they had used to manage their feelings in childhood and suggest how therapists can make use of this information. Then we describe ways of coping with feelings in adulthood. We only describe strategies that participants articulated to us, even though they probably used strategies they were not able to describe. Children are largely unaware of how they are coping with feelings, so their memories and reports of this complex area of psychological functioning inevitably represent a limited truth. Nonetheless, our participants gave us interesting and important information about this process. Throughout, we continue to draw implications for psychotherapists.

MANAGING FEELINGS IN CHILDHOOD

When we looked at participants' descriptions of the ways they had managed their emotions in childhood, several categories emerged. It is important to emphasize that the categories were derived from the interview material. They were not developed to reflect our views on defenses, cognitive styles, or other formulations about strategies for managing feelings. The categories include, in order of frequency of use, acting on emotions, distancing from feelings, experiencing or expressing feelings, hiding emotions from other people, using fantasy to manage feelings, behavioral coping or self-soothing, seeking out other people for comfort or other relational strategies, avoiding, beginning to develop cognitive strategies, and using humor.

Our participants varied in the number of strategies they employed. For example, Felicia used seven out of these ten strategies in childhood, whereas several participants described using only two.

Although being able to use a variety of emotional coping strategies helped these women be less vulnerable as children and later, more was not always better. Here we discuss each of these methods, beginning with the ones most frequently used.

Taking Action

The most common method the women used to handle emotions in childhood was to take action to release the tension of the feeling; all but two described having done this. At times acting was a creative and productive outlet for the emotions; at other times acting was self-destructive. We suggest that most of the actions they took in childhood to manage their feelings had both constructive and destructive elements. Thompson and Calkins (1996) believe this is an inevitable consequence of the complex compromises children in abusive or neglectful families must make in the way they regulate their emotions. They must try to maximize the nurturance they can obtain while minimizing their risks of harm.

In some of our participants' narratives the action was predominantly helpful or constructive, but in some that was less evident. Occasionally the actions were conscious expressions of internal experience; as children they usually were not aware of such meanings. Darlene described an incident when she was a young adolescent in which her mother wouldn't let her go to a Broadway play with the church minister, and she expressed her feelings through actions:

> I said, "Why can't I go?" And she said, "Well, I don't really know him," because I was going to a different church than the family church. And she said, "He could be a pervert, for all I know. He could do anything to you." And that really ticked me off because I felt like she can see it in all these other people. And that was the one time she refused to let me do something. And it really made me angry. I went in and broke an expensive mirror in the house. [Interviewer: Did you get in trouble?] No.

She ignored that it even happened. I threw the hairbrush directly at it and it shattered and I left it there and it was never mentioned.

When Darlene described the incident, she knew that she had been representing her anger in action; she may not have known that at the time. We view the incident as constructive because it was a way of having and expressing a very real, powerful, and (to us) appropriate feeling. After all, her mother was not keeping her safe from perverts in the family yet was depriving her of an opportunity on the outside chance that this man might abuse her. The action can also be seen as destructive because it is impulsive. It is not certain that Darlene as a young adolescent was able to choose whether or not to break the mirror. The incident could have led her to have fears about her self-control, and breaking things was unlikely to have led to any helpful resolution of the problem.

A therapist listening to such an anecdote in therapy would want to explore many aspects of the client's feelings and thoughts about the incident. How does she view it as an adult? What does she think about the fact that her mother did not say anything about it? What did she learn from that event? A psychotherapist would have concerns about a client who continued to use action as a response to anger in adulthood and might talk about other alternatives. At the same time the therapist might let the client know that at the time she threw the brush she had few alternatives. However, a therapist hearing the story from a client who is greatly inhibited in her expression of anger might wonder if she had learned to fear the destructive quality of that anger from her childhood experience.

Other participants recalled acting self-destructively as a means of managing feelings of pain and rage as a child. Beth used to scratch her legs until they bled. Helen and Galen described cutting themselves and using alcohol and various substances to manage their feelings. However, while Helen said she used alcohol and cutting to numb her feelings, Galen described the same actions as a way she could break through her numbness. "[I was] feeling this intense rage and directing it toward myself [and I was] . . . so numbed out that I just had to do something physical to get back into my body, like it's an entrance way or something. If I see my blood, I know I am in pain. Because no one is validating my pain and I want to have physical hurt. . . . And it does take away the numbness." Similarly, Elena as a child used crises and exciting (and sometimes dangerous) challenges to break through her own numbness.

It is not surprising that children try to manage intense and essentially unmanageable feelings through action. Therapists working with children with abuse histories can help them by exploring the meanings associated with these actions, validating their feelings, supporting their need to have some physical means of expression of those feelings, and helping them find constructive outlets for that energy.

Distancing

In childhood, the next most common method of managing emotions described by this group was to distance themselves from their feelings. (We see dissociation as a type of distancing and sometimes use the terms interchangeably.) This type of strategy involved *internally* putting some distance between their conscious experience and the related feelings. Often this involved "numbing," "trying not to care," or telling themselves not to feel this. Almost every participant described some version of that. Sometimes they did this to manage their feelings related specifically to the abuse. Felicia said that when she was being abused, "I just kind of shut down after [the abuse]. . . . When the episode would happen, I'd get through it and sort of like put it out of my mind. . . . But it was always something gnawing me. And I knew what it was but I almost couldn't verbalize it right. What I think, I made a split somewhere in my mind, and when it was going on I sort of went away, you know? And that's how I handled it."

Splitting off a part of themselves was a common method of dealing with intense and hard-to-manage feelings. Carrie said, "I think

I used to look at the pictures on the wall; I think I used to sing to myself sometimes. . . . I think there are a lot of different things that I did to try to deal with it when I was little; I split off—basically it wasn't happening to me. So it happened to someone else in a way." Felicia talked of "going away" into a peaceful place inside herself, "like a little vacation from things."

Sometimes they did not entirely disconnect from parts of themselves but distanced themselves from their feelings in a less extreme way. Janet described it this way: "I used to dissociate on a regular basis in my childhood. I would be sitting at the dinner table and I wouldn't be there. All the voices seemed far. . . . I felt far away. There was this fog in me. That used to happen to me regularly, that I would feel like I was in another dimension. It happened throughout elementary school. I just can remember feeling I didn't know how to connect back."

Janet's example also points out her awareness of the cost of this technique, which was the inability to connect back. These examples show that the women used these strategies to gain some distance from intolerable feelings like pain and rage. Under the circumstances, dissociating seemed relatively adaptive when compared, for example, to using substances to gain distance from their feelings. (Recently, clinical researchers have argued about the costs and benefits of dissociation at the time of a traumatic experience [van der Kolk, van der Hart, and Marmar, 1996].)

Our perspective is that children have few ways to manage traumatic feelings. Dissociation and other forms of distancing help some children survive. As therapists, we remind clients of this fact and then help them find ways to stop dissociating in their adult lives.

Experiencing and Expressing

In the course of the interviews, a number of the women told us about their childhood experiences of expressing their feelings directly or being determined to have the feeling, even if they did not feel safe enough to express it. For example, when Darlene's grandmother died, she expressed how she was feeling but also had to "shut off" her grieving because of the family rules about not showing emotion. She remembered: "I was crying, I was hysterical. . . . And then people were saying, 'Well, you have to be strong for your mother, you have to be strong for your mother, and you don't cry.' And those kind of things, which I just was not prepared to deal with in that way." Darlene then went on to experience (and express) her grief by not speaking for six months because overt expression was not tolerated in her family.

Felicia had a similar experience of being committed to having her feelings, even though expression was not always possible. She described listening to music to connect with her emotions: "Because, I wouldn't show emotion, but what I would do, when I was listening to the music, I could see it and feel it and hear it inside, and I was releasing it a little bit at a time. Because I think had I not had that, I would just have exploded. So that was a little valve to release. And sometimes I would cry for a song. And that was my only way of releasing it."

It is no surprise that the direct expression of emotion was intolerable in the families of these women. Because they felt unsafe expressing their feelings, they often honored the integrity of their emotions while they were alone. We see our participants' resolve as children to experience and express their feelings as reflecting significant resiliency and as indicating their commitment to remaining whole. We encourage therapists of trauma survivors to notice any evidence that their clients had tried in childhood to maintain their feelings, however unwelcome they were in the family, and help these clients appreciate this evidence of their resiliency.

Hiding Feelings

Several participants described themselves as children who intentionally hid their feelings from other people (often with good cause, in our view). It was not safe for these women to express their distress because it was not tolerated in their families or in their broader social worlds. Even as children, they told us, they knew that deliberately hiding their emotions from other people was an act of self-preservation. For example, when we asked Darlene if she preferred to be alone or with others when she was upset as a child, she responded, "By myself, because I hated for people to see me cry. I hated to cry and hated to be seen crying. . . . And I also think, I began to prefer to be by myself when I realized that even if people noticed that I was upset, they weren't going to do anything about it." She also reported that in her family, "crying was a real sign of weakness, like you don't cry. It's not really necessary. It doesn't get you anyplace and it doesn't solve anything." Thus the family intolerance of tears and her awareness that no one would comfort or protect her combined to make Darlene choose not to show her feelings as a child.

Felicia also felt that showing her emotions would be harmful to her and therefore decided to hide her feelings. "I wouldn't cry. If people would try to hurt me, I just wouldn't show the hurt. . . . I was like a stone face. I remember a teacher I didn't get along with. She said a few things that hurt me, but I didn't show any emotion. I didn't want her to know that it hurt me."

Both of the African American women who had grown up in urban families felt it necessary to hide their vulnerable feelings, as opposed to some of the other participants who had suppressed their anger. We see the difference between strategically keeping your feelings to yourself and never developing the capacity to express an emotion out of terror of the consequences. We are tempted to speculate on the role of culture here, but our interviews can only suggest this area for further exploration. A therapist working with clients growing up in dangerous urban areas or urban African American clients might notice whether particularly vulnerable thoughts and feelings needed to be hidden.

Overall, these examples and others in which participants hid their feelings when they were young portray children and youth who knew what was safe and acceptable in their families. As far as we can tell from their stories and from our work with clients with trauma histories, they were correct in thinking that their families did not welcome and would not respond to their feelings. However, survivors often think their perceptions are invalid. Therapists can help by pointing out that they were probably seeing things clearly and that it was adaptive to hide their feelings. The work survivors need to do, of course, is to learn how their adult worlds are different—probably safer and more receptive—and to find ways to stop hiding in this different context.

Fantasy

Several participants described using the realm of thought and fantasy to regulate emotions. In a wonderful and rich example, Anne recalled:

> We had a lot of pretend that we did together. We had dollhouse people we played with all the time. They had lives of their own. And we had Jacco Jeep. Jacco Jeep was a bad man who did awful things to our dolls when we were away from home. We were scared to leave them. So we usually took them with us. And when we went to Canada once, we needed birth certificates for all of them. Because we heard if you went to Canada and didn't have a birth certificate, you couldn't get back. So all of our dolls had birth certificates. We crumpled them up so they'd look old.

Ilona too described using fantasy to manage her childhood feelings and to create a sense of self: "I loved to read, I loved music, I loved movies. I wanted to grow up to be Alice Fay or Betty Grable; it was that immersing myself that helped me salvage me as a person. . . . Otherwise God only knows what would have happened to me." Carrie told us with some embarrassment about a wonderful fantasy that helped get her through. She explained:

I made up a personality. Do you remember, there's a car-
toon, it's Mr. Peabody? Mr. Peabody is this dog; it was
really smart, and I think that they had some kind of a
time-travel machine. So what I did was I identified with
this character. I was fairly smart, so I could identify with
this dog, this little, smart little dog, and he travels
through time. And I just had this story in my head where
Peabody was this healthy part of myself, smart and kind
of together and able to handle things. And basically the
story that I made up was that at a certain point Peabody
left. She just went away. And the idea was that when
things were better she would come back and save me.

The fantasy expresses Carrie's hopefulness that someday things
would get better so Mr. Peabody could return. In their important
book on resiliency, Tedeschi and Calhoun (1995) also emphasize
the role of hope in resilient reactions to trauma.

Fantasy sometimes involved thinking about actions, which then
provided an alternative to having to *do* something. For example, a
number of our participants *thought* about running away but didn't.
We assume there was some comfort for them in this thought, much
as some survivors think about suicide as a way of feeling they have
some alternatives to tolerating intolerable feelings.

We see the use of fantasy as an enormously resilient method
some children have of dealing with their feelings, working them
over, envisioning a better place and a better time in their lives, and
sometimes sharing in that process with someone else, especially
other abused siblings. Such a creative use of the imagination needs
to be acknowledged and appreciated by therapists, who can then
help their clients find other ways to express their evident creativity. Therapists for children and adults can help clients enlarge and
enrich their fantasy lives by inviting imagery and encouraging other
forms of creative expression that can hold and soothe traumatic
feelings.

Behavioral Coping (Self-Soothing)

Only two women, Anne and Felicia, described specific methods of soothing themselves in childhood. Anne sang to herself. "I knew that—'Cinderella, Cinderella, mop the ocean, dust the stars and mop the ocean, the hinges on the fringes in Heaven need adjusting.' I knew all those words. I would sing all of that when I was feeling. . . . If 'Annie' had been around when I was little, I am sure I would have known every word to every song from 'Annie.'" As described earlier, Felicia used music to soothe herself and connect with her feelings.

In addition to reading, which many of our participants relied on as children, others may have had different methods of self-soothing that they were unable to remember and describe many years later. And many victims of abuse have great difficulty finding safe and satisfying methods of soothing themselves. This is an important area of focus for therapists, who need to spend significant time in therapy helping clients find or invent such techniques.

Relational Strategies

Getting help from other people to deal with hard feelings in childhood was also rare among this group of women—for good reasons, we think, as we hear and understand their histories. For many, there were no safe people to turn to with the full intensity of their emotions. Yet several of the women found a way to use other people in a limited way to help them with some of their feelings. Anne described using other people as a buffer to protect her from her mother, who was a primary source of pain in her life. She said, "Having other people around was an insulation, and I think my mother tended to behave better when there were more people around. Or I would try and get out of there and go to [other people], go visit friends, or get on the phone." Carrie was able to express many of her feelings to her mother and would seek out her mother for comfort, except for feelings related to the abuse by her father.

Seeking out other people for comfort is an important skill, but this strategy depends on supportive people being available and is best complemented by a strategy of self-reliance that gives options for managing feelings. For child and adult survivors who never learned to get help from others, and in fact learned that it was not safe, developing a sense of trust and skill in doing so is vital to their recovery. In her doctoral dissertation, Jessica Goldstein (1998) found that adult abuse survivors who described themselves as reaching out to others for emotional support were doing significantly better than those who tended not to turn to others.

Avoiding

Darlene described herself as a child trying to control her environment so nothing would happen that would lead to painful feelings. She avoided situations that she knew would cause some form of distress, and she tried never to do anything wrong "out of terror of being beaten." This strategy preserved her physical well-being. In another instance, when several cousins who were perpetrators of her abuse showed up at her house, Darlene recalled, "I think I just ran upstairs or something because I didn't want to be in the middle of stuff." In this example, we see Darlene as remarkably resilient in finding a way to avoid painful feelings and also physical harm. Again, we suspect other women in our sample did that when they were young but did not remember it in a way they could describe to us. Child and adult clients can be helped to think through when avoidance is a useful strategy and when it interferes with other goals.

Cognitive Strategies

This category includes using thoughts to manage feelings. For example, some people talk to themselves to make themselves feel better; they try to understand a situation in order to decrease the emotions involved; they learn about feelings and how to cope with them. Only one participant, Felicia, explicitly described using cognitive strategies as a child, but a number used reading to help them under-

stand and manage their feelings. Felicia told us she talked to herself, telling herself that bad things happen to people but you have
to go on. She remembered seeing a sign on someone's desk that said
something to the effect that this moment will pass. She said she told
herself, "It's not going to be like this all the time." And she said, "I
remembered that; I knew that bad things would happen, and even
happy things, even happy moments will pass. Nothing is going to
stay forever the same way. So I saw that as well. Opportunities will
come my way. When I'm old enough, I'll get out of here."

That contains amazing wisdom for a child. In fact many of our
participants' stories reflect unusual maturity and perspective.

Felicia remembered trying to figure out relationships: "So I tried
to read a book about couples. Like *Patience and Sarah*, I read that
book, and that helped me a lot, because it was two women inter-
acting. They were a couple. And I really loved that book; I learned
a lot about how sometimes things don't go right in a relationship,
but if you're honest and try to be open, you try to just deal with
things without hurting but trying to get what you need and have
the person get to what they need."

Although Felicia was the only woman to describe a use of cognitive strategies in childhood, we are confident that many others
had done so but could not tell us about it directly. For example,
Janet said that, besides praying, "I'd just fantasize about how I'd get
out, how could I leave, how could I run away. . . . And then as I got
older, I knew my ticket out was to go away to college. And that gave
me some hopefulness about it. At least I knew I could get out of
there." Although she was telling us it was a fantasy, it was also a
thought—that someday she would leave—that helped her survive
her awful childhood.

A number of the women told us how reading helped them get
through. Galen relied on reading to help her understand her experiences and manage her feelings: "When I was a teenager, I would read
Nietzsche and Tolstoy, like real grim stuff, but it was on paper. And
it did make sense and it validated my reality, I think, in a lot of ways."

Many of these examples came from adolescence, and we believe that these strategies are developmentally dependent on cognitive maturation. The fact that we received no reports of our survivors having used cognitive strategies in childhood raises some questions about the usefulness of trying to teach such strategies to children. However, as we have said, they might have used these methods earlier but were unable to describe them. Certainly, therapists of adolescent clients can fruitfully encourage the use of a variety of cognitive strategies to manage traumatic feelings.

Humor

Anne alone used humor to reframe at least some of the painful events in her childhood so they could be seen as funny. Humor was prevalent among her family members. She said, "I think that saved a lot of situations, and actually it's a gift that my parents gave us because their humor through tough times was extraordinary. . . . I was thinking about why I'm not in an insane asylum somewhere. And I think humor has to be a big part of it."

Although therapists can encourage child clients to use humor to manage feelings, they need to be careful not to appear to be in any way minimizing the traumatic experiences or associated feelings. One of the wonderful gifts trauma survivors can give each other is a kind of gallows humor that no one without such a history would come up with or appreciate; nor could anyone without such a history safely make humorous comments to a survivor without risking misunderstanding and hurt feelings.

Therapeutic Implications of Childhood Methods of Managing Feelings

A number of important therapeutic implications emerge from what we learned about the ways our participants managed their feelings in childhood. One distinguishing feature among methods was the extent to which feelings remained in consciousness. Expressing or experiencing feelings directly, getting help from others, having feelings but hiding them from others, and self-soothing all left the participants in touch with their feelings. In contrast, distancing from feelings (numbing, shutting down, and so forth) and some forms of acting out involved not being aware of the emotions. Acting out and acting in—somatizing—are methods of coping with feelings that a person may not be aware of. Participants did not tell us about somatizing as a method of managing feelings, presumably because they would not have been aware that this was a method they were using, even if they were. (Traumatized children often initially come to clinical settings with somatic complaints.)

In the long run, our participants had a harder time when they were not in touch with their feelings. We encourage therapists to think clearly about what methods of feeling management their clients are describing, including their stories from childhood, and help clients understand why they had behaved the way they did. So often clients are globally ashamed of their behaviors in the past and have no understanding of why they might have done what they did or what psychological problem they were attempting to solve with their behavior. Having a framework for understanding diminishes shame and enormously enhances individuals' capacity to use their intelligence to understand themselves in their histories.

Another important implication is the connection between distancing from and acting on feeling in childhood. The relationship between these two methods is amazingly obvious and bi-directional in our interviews. For our participants, keeping their emotions out of consciousness often led to a variety of actions that were driven by the underlying feelings. Further, certain kinds of actions were used to keep particular feelings out of awareness. In these traumatized children, whose cognitive skills were not fully developed, these two strategies were heavily relied upon because of limited internal and external resources. Again, an important therapeutic task is to help clients understand this connection and begin to appreciate the cost of defensive tactics that eliminate feelings from awareness.

Our strongest therapeutic implication relates to the importance of the therapist understanding what methods her client, whether child or adult, is using or did use in childhood to deal with feelings. The psychotherapist can apply that knowledge to helping the client understand how these coping mechanisms have influenced her behavior, both in positive ways and in ways that have been less constructive for her. Clients need validation for the strategies they selected, which were often the best strategies available to them, given the context of their lives and the risks and resources they had to work with. They also need to learn why those strategies may no longer serve them and to understand why that is so.

Some childhood strategies suggest particular strengths that should be nurtured in clients. The use of fantasy in particular suggests a kind of creativity that can lead to the development of other creative outlets for expressing and managing traumatic feelings; the ability to reach out to others also shows significant resiliency and should be honored as such and developed. Therapists working with clients who indicate that they used cognitive strategies in childhood need to appreciate the extent to which that reflects a major resource for the work of recovery in adulthood.

MANAGING FEELINGS IN ADULTHOOD

We have much more information about the way our participants managed their emotions in adulthood, partly because we talked to them as adults and it was easier for them to remember and describe their methods. Also, adults have a greater range and more elaborate ways of managing their feelings than children. We started with participants' own descriptions of how they managed emotions while they were talking about specific feelings and then looked for similarities among the methods. Many of the categories were the same as those described in childhood, but several others emerged. The strategies were, in order of frequency of use, using cognitive strategies, experiencing and expressing feelings, coping behaviorally, distancing or numbing, avoiding triggers, using relational strategies, taking action, hiding feelings from others, somatizing, using diversionary tactics, using humor, and practicing spirituality.

Cognitive Strategies

One of the two methods most frequently described was the use of cognitive strategies. This included managing strong and difficult feelings by talking to themselves, thinking about themselves and others in ways that helped make their pain more tolerable (for example, thinking about other people who are in more pain), reading about trauma and healing to better understand the process, and regulating potentially destructive impulses by interposing thought between the impulse and action, to list the most common.

Several participants described talking to themselves as a helpful way to manage feelings; some used this technique to help with memories and flashbacks. Carrie talked about a way of allowing herself to know she was having these feelings but reminding herself that the feelings were really from the past.

Felicia told us about how she talked herself through the research interviews: "So what I've learned to do—when I float is because I'm scared. And I don't think I have to be afraid of the both of you. It's my old way of responding to fear, I guess. This is the dialogue that was going on in my head. I said, 'Yeah, you're floating, you're a little afraid, but really there's nothing to be afraid of. The study is going to help people, just try to keep open and go on with it.'"

Learning to engage in reality-oriented self-talk can be extremely helpful to clients and should be actively encouraged by therapists. Often the self-talk that already exists in survivors is self-denigrating, abusive, and distorted, so an early step in learning to use this strategy adaptively is for the client to learn to discriminate inner-child voices from her adult voice. Then she can use that adult voice to help all parts of her perceive a situation accurately and respond appropriately.

Some participants used what social psychologist Shelley Taylor has described as "downward social comparisons" to help them cope with their overwhelming feelings. As Taylor (1983) describes it, this involves reassuring oneself that other people have greater difficulties and so it is not necessary to feel so bad. Elena reported, "No matter how awful I feel or how many things are going wrong or that I'm tired of having memories or that I wish sex weren't the way it is sometimes, my life today is better than most people's lives ever get, and I know that." Although research evidence supports the usefulness of downward comparisons for trauma survivors, psychotherapists should be careful about suggesting it because, as with humor, it can appear to clients as though the therapist is minimizing the client's victimization.

Several participants who were aware of strong tendencies to act out in damaging ways were in the process of developing their ability to impose thought between emotion and action. Galen struggled with addiction and a tendency to act impulsively and destructively. She described trying to recognize her feelings and understand where they were coming from instead of acting them out. For example, she sometimes felt rage toward a client who terrorized people in the halfway house where she worked: "I just feel like I hate him sometimes, like I hate my father. Sometimes, suddenly, I'll feel like hitting someone or kicking something, or something like that. I just think about it and let the feeling pass." Galen also described the strategy of talking to herself. An important lesson she had learned is that feelings change: "I thought that the feeling was never going to end, that I would feel this way forever. And I feel like I've learned that, no matter how bad I feel, that the feeling is going to pass. And that other feelings are going to come in, too, like that I'm going to feel joy, I'm going to feel faith, I'm going to feel hope. And I think that really keeps me going."

Helen also was learning how to use her thinking to manage her cutting and substance abuse. She noticed that she could say to herself, if she felt like going home and cutting herself, "No, not now." Helen was in the early stage of getting through one day at a time to manage her cutting and substance abuse and was using the ideas she was learning in therapy and in AA to help her through the moments of intense emotions.

Most likely, the fact that so many of our participants use cognitive strategies reflects our selection process. We required that all participants be in therapy, which often teaches such an approach. Galen and Helen seem to us to have been compelled to develop skills in using cognitive strategies to deal with destructive elements in their lives: their strong addictions and tendency for impulsive acting out. More generally, people's ability to think and to understand and to influence their actions and feelings are powerful tools they bring to the process of recovery from trauma. Therapists who work with trauma survivors should never underestimate the value of those tools. Although some trauma therapists focus exclusively on cognition and behavior, even therapists who work much more with clients' feelings need to emphasize the cognitive components of recovery.

Experiencing and Expressing

Experiencing feelings and expressing them were described by almost all participants and were interrelated, so we put them into the same category. Most of the women talked about experiencing and expressing their feelings; others were more focused on one or the other. Many had first learned to let themselves sit with the emotions, then to express themselves in constructive ways except in potentially harmful situations. The process of learning to express feelings also involves learning to choose when to express them. Often, traumatized individuals have difficulty experiencing the intensity of their feelings, and they rely heavily on dissociation to manage that intensity. Moreover, even nontraumatized women have to learn to develop their voices and express how they feel, despite strong societal prohibitions. Thus, this set of emotional strategies is complicated both by the intensity and shame associated with trauma and by the general social bias against any expression of difficult feelings by women.

Some of the women talked about experiencing and expressing their emotions in general. For example, Carrie noted, "I would say I've gotten pretty good at, if something is bothering me, to say it or even if something is making me angry to say it, and I think that my friends feel that it's something they can tell me if they are angry about something." Carrie had reached a sophisticated level of being able to tolerate and express her own feelings, as well as being comfortable with other people's expression of feeling. A goal of much therapeutic work is to help clients represent their feelings when they arise in ways that do not rupture their connections with others but, in fact, deepen them.

Sometimes the feelings associated with traumatic events are so overwhelming that experiencing their full intensity is too frightening. After Darlene was raped in an elevator as an adult, she noticed:

> I was totally numbed out after that, because I didn't tell anyone for a while and just didn't deal with it or tried to ignore that it had happened. Then I went through a period when I minimized it, and I was telling someone and they said something like, "God, that's awful! You were raped!" And I said, "Well, it wasn't a rape." So I went through that phase, and it took a while before I let myself then feel sad that it happened. Because I was afraid that I would just start feeling really sad, and I would get really depressed and get lost in that. But then, eventually, I did get really sad because it happened and, then I know I got angry and I became rageful.

So initially Darlene was not able to experience her feelings at all. Then she began to feel, first in a minimized form, and then fully. Eventually she was able to express them to her therapists, her friends, and us.

Several of the women talked about the process of learning to acknowledge their feelings and beginning to express them. Helen, for example, noticed: "I'm more free if I just say how I feel. Sometimes people are uncomfortable with that, but at least I say how I feel. But in some places I won't say." She also was aware that she was beginning to experience her feelings more immediately. "I feel the feelings I'm supposed to feel that same night (after therapy), so it's getting closer." We encourage therapists to help their clients notice the time lapse between being in a situation and having the associated feelings. Typically with healing and new learning in therapy, the time lapse gets smaller. Noticing that progress is often heartening to clients and therapists.

Ilona was more focused on expressing her feelings after years of burying them. She talked about the importance of expressing in the interviews "all the hurt and the pain and the rage" that she has felt. In her life with her husband, Ilona often had angry outbursts with him, and she felt, "I've had to fight over the years to have those feelings accepted. . . . And I would say to him, 'You've got to understand, I am entitled to my feelings.'"

Our view of this is different from Ilona's. We believe that expression by itself, without the capacity to tolerate and experience the feelings, is not necessarily helpful. Jessica Goldstein (1998) found that women who said they used "venting feelings" as a coping style were doing significantly less well than women using other approaches, particularly turning to others for support. The task for trauma survivors is to be able to experience their feelings and express them when and only when it is appropriate and safe for them to do so.

Experiencing and expressing feelings are very important processes for trauma survivors—processes central to their recovery. All of our participants had struggled with being able to do this, and all indicated their growing ability to do so. We see resiliency in their commitment to having all of their feelings and in the determination with which they persist in the learning process, which is always difficult. Much time is spent in good therapy developing these skills. This work needs to be very concrete, considering specific situations and the feelings that were aroused and exploring with clients what they might have said to represent their feelings in a way that did not needlessly or unhelpfully disrupt the social context.

Behavioral Coping (Self-Soothing)

Behavioral coping is another deliberate strategy that is often learned in therapy; it was used by eight of our participants. Janet articulately described the essence of behavioral coping: "I meditate, I exercise, I even do some kind of yoga, because I feel the difference. When I don't I get more stressed, and I'm vulnerable to the raw emotions, when I don't take care of my needs like that." Other participants reported a variety of behavioral strategies such as exercising; watching their food, caffeine, and alcohol intake; reading books; writing poetry; or keeping a journal.

Elena participated in Model Mugging, a self-defense program that helps individuals learn how to protect themselves against physical attack by increasing their protective awareness, using their voices, and having them practice techniques against real men in protective padding. She explained why she took the workshop: "One of the reasons I did Model Mugging is because no matter what I think, now I know I can protect myself. Because if it happens I know what to do, my body knows what to do. When I did Model Mugging, I did it because I was afraid on the street." Taking the course was a form of behavioral coping, which resulted in feelings of greater inner safety and comfort.

Most of our participants used methods of behavioral coping, and many had learned to do that in their therapies. These methods represent a set of options that psychotherapists sometimes do not consider in their work with clients but that can be powerful aids to recovery. We encourage therapists to familiarize themselves with these options, refer clients to them, and then use clients' reports of their experiences in the psychotherapy.

Distancing and Numbing

Distancing and numbing are strategies used to manage emotions by either not feeling them or lessening their intensity. This can happen consciously or unconsciously. Eight participants described this process. When asked in the initial interview about whether she had ever felt rejected by someone, Carrie could not remember any instances. She went on to explain why she thought she wasn't remembering: "I think I probably have a hard time with rejection, and I think I use a lot of denial, I deny my vulnerability. And, truthfully, I'm sitting here, and I don't really know you guys very well, and I think that what I tend to do is stuff my vulnerable feelings. And so it's hard for me to connect right now with times when I felt rejected." We suspect she was right, and we view her self-knowledge as an important aspect of her resiliency.

One mechanism commonly used by traumatized women is to compartmentalize feelings—a form of dissociation. Elena described how a part of her, Ely, helps her manage some of her feelings: "Part of [going into therapy] was Ely wanting to say something. And I wouldn't, because I know enough to know that she was the source of pain, or she was the repository of pain and knowledge that I didn't want to have."

Helen described such extensive compartmentalization and so little communication between those cut-off parts that we initially thought she might have dissociative identity disorder (formerly called multiple personality disorder). She told us at the follow-up interview that she had also wondered, but the various mental health professionals she had worked with had decided she did not. In any case she described one experience she sometimes had of compartmentalization: "Every now and then a door will open and I can look in and see what's going on there, and sometimes the feelings will just take over. But there are some closets that haven't been opened yet; there's some things I haven't seen yet. I get glimpses of it, like the door opens for a second and shuts. . . . It's mostly the feelings that are multiple or whatever you want to call it, and only in small doses."

Some women go numb in response to intense emotions or when they are in a place where it doesn't feel safe to experience their feelings. Felicia said, "I don't really like to talk about my childhood that much to people. Because first of all, it wasn't a pretty sight, and it wasn't happy. And even now when people ask me about my childhood, my whole body gets numb, and then I float." When Galen was working with disturbed adolescent girls, she noticed, "I did used to shut down and become numb. I would just have to go through the motions of the things that I needed to do to keep the kids safe or whatever, and then later have my feelings."

Although distancing and numbing are life-saving techniques for children who are being abused, when these methods are generalized and become major strategies for coping with adult life, they can interfere with healthy adaptation. One of the consequences of distancing and numbing we see in our participants is that the feelings being avoided erupt in some other way. Therapists need to teach clients about the normal and adaptive aspects of these methods of surviving traumatic experiences and help them find ways that work better for their adult lives.

Avoiding Triggers

Six participants described avoiding triggers, which means deciding to stay away from people, places, things, or situations that are reminiscent of the trauma. Often this means avoiding intimate relationships, one's family of origin, and certain types of work. Beth remarked, "I tend to avoid. I have avoided intimacy because it means there's going to be a lot of pain and a lot of fear that will cancel out any enjoyment there is." Clearly, there is a cost to such a strategy, but it can be an effective way to manage some kinds of feelings.

Darlene commented, "When I came to college in 1980, I knew I would never go back to [my hometown], because I always get depressed when I go there, so I hate going there and I avoid it." It is important to add that when we interviewed Darlene six years later, she was living in her mother's house in her hometown, to convalesce from a serious illness; she was not at all triggered by the experience. Her experience offers a helpful reminder to both clients and therapists that the way they feel, and the steps they need to take to manage those feelings at one stage of their recovery, is not likely the way they will always be. These things change with growth and healing.

Deciding to avoid triggering situations can be a helpful strategy that involves knowing oneself and making choices on the basis of that knowledge. Often before clients can take this step, they need first to learn that they are being triggered when they have intense and intrusive feelings and second to notice what circumstances cause the trigger. Avoiding some triggers will interfere with life goals, and clients may choose to learn to deal with these reactions. For example, being triggered by sexual feelings in a dating situation can lead a survivor to avoid dating, which then interferes with the commitment to marry and have children. However, a person triggered by violent movies may well choose to avoid seeing such movies.

Relational Strategies

As we have said, few of our participants used relational strategies in childhood that involved reaching out to others for help or invoked an internal representation of a supportive relationship in the face of difficult feelings. At the time of the initial interviews, half were able to do this; all had learned to do so by the time of the follow-up interviews. Carrie and Beth made the most use of both internal and external relational strategies. Carrie described at length how she has "learned that talking to people helps a lot. And it's much better to talk about things. It makes you feel a lot better ultimately. It's not good to keep all this stuff inside. I think that's what got my father into trouble to begin with."

Initially, Beth told us, she thought of her son. "My son has kept me going. Even now when things just feel really bleak, I think about him and about that relationship because that's a real, real important thing in my life."

Turning to others for help in managing feelings can undoubtedly be a strong and constructive coping method. Survivors probably need to have had significant helpful relationships in the past if they are to be able to do it. Positive relational experiences in therapy can also make this strategy possible, as Olio and Cornell (1993) suggest, and in one way or another all of our participants could do so by the time of the follow-up interviews. During the course of psychotherapy, survivor clients need encouragement and coaching, first to dare to explore relational methods and then to develop their skills in these interactions.

Action

Four of the women described using action in adulthood as a means of expressing their feelings. In some instances, action was used as a deliberate and constructive outlet for emotions. Elena described how she intentionally vented her anger toward her father: "I smashed one of the photos of him until I cracked the glass in the [family] montage. And I've left it that way. It was very pleasing to me. . . . I smashed this thing until it cracked, and then I smashed it some more. And I just loved it." Elena found an action that, for her, expressed her rage better than words could.

However, several women talked about the risk in impulsively acting out their feelings rather than doing it deliberately. For example, Ilona mentioned several incidents in which she threw objects in the direction of—but not quite at—family members. Janet also described hitting her husband in the heat of an argument. These participants' awareness of their potential for acting out violently and their sense of the risks to themselves and their relationships of such actions, are their best defenses against its developing into a pattern. The impulsive, destructive examples that the women gave us all occurred when they were feeling threatened and then became enraged.

After considerable uncertainty about how to classify it, we decided to categorize self-abuse as a form of action. Helen was one of several participants who described using self-abuse as a way to manage her rage. She said that when she was furious with someone, "I just wanted to rip their heads off or something like that, but now it's just I know where it's coming from so I mostly direct it at myself." Helen is describing a developmental process of learning how to manage her rage, from acting it out to turning it inward. Clearly, self-abuse is not an optimal strategy, but for these women it was at times a safer alternative than direct expression. Sometimes it was also a precursor to learning more adaptive ways of handling rage.

Acting on feelings is often a complex and problematic strategy for adult survivors. When it is out of their control, it tends to frighten and shame them and thus cannot be considered helpful. It is hard to think of self-abuse as adaptive, although at times our participants described it as preferable to previous ways of dealing with their rage, and we think it needs to be considered in that light. Occasionally, acting on feelings can be a deliberate means of expression and for some survivors can be helpful. Therapists need to think hard about the meaning and context of action for a particular client before deciding how to respond to such reports.

Hiding Feelings from Other People

Four participants told us about hiding their feelings from other people in adulthood as a way of managing their feelings. The women varied in how often they used this strategy. Galen described a specific situation at work, where she hid her fear from a person who reminded her of her father. Felicia relied heavily on this strategy as a way of being in the world. In between these two extremes were Beth and Ilona. Beth described hiding only her sad feelings from other people: "I guess a lot of my life, I've kind of had this inner person and this outer person, and the outer person wouldn't cry, but this inner person would curl up and cry." Ilona noticed how hard it is for her to say no to some people. "There are still situations in my life that I find very difficult to say, 'This is unacceptable.' For me, it would be just as easy to blend into the woodwork, disappear, put a smile on my face, and say, 'That's okay,' when it's like, 'You son of a bitch, get out of my face!'"

Although our participants did not describe many instances of hiding their feelings, from our clinical work with survivors we assume they probably hid often but were not aware of it. We have seen in therapies that some clients are reluctant to learn about their own feelings, or experience them, for fear that they must then express them to the object of those feelings. For such clients, learning that they can hide their feelings—that it is possible to have a strong feeling and choose to keep it to themselves—can be an important step toward becoming free to feel and acknowledge those feelings. Focusing on the development of this skill in therapy can be an important step in recovery.

Somatizing

Several participants talked about how certain feelings are often associated with certain somatic complaints. This probably happens in some of the other women, but they were not as aware of it and so could not tell us about it. Beth noticed, "My emotions kind of go into my head and then I get headaches, and then I'm not dealing with the sadness or the pain. . . . Then [I] worked out and felt sadness again and no headache." This is a good example of using behavioral coping to address the physical and the emotional pain. Felicia, who was plagued by conversion reactions, described them: "It's like a frozen state, and my face and arms feel like I'm frozen but not cold, you know what I mean? Really hard to move, and all of my senses are heightened, light, sound. Almost like a panic; I guess panic sets in. I had very low, depressed states and the conversions would set in during those times."

Helen talked about her asthma. "My dog died. [The cult demanded I kill my dog.] The way I look at that, my asthma is a defense, so that I won't get close to animals." Janet also described getting tension headaches, particularly after visiting her family of origin.

It is known that somatic reactions are very common responses to childhood sexual abuse. Therapists working with survivors need to be mindful of the likelihood that their clients are having physical problems, which they may or may not be talking about in therapy. Further, those problems may well have psychological aspects and need attention both from a physician and from the psychotherapist. Somatization is even more likely in cultures or subcultures in which psychological symptoms are not accepted or acknowledged. Over time, clients can be taught to interpret the language of their bodies so they can begin to focus on the traumatic emotions and experiences expressed by many somatic symptoms. Often once this is done, the symptoms lessen or disappear.

Diversionary Tactics

Several participants described using what we call diversionary tactics. This strategy involves distracting oneself from painful or intolerable feelings to regulate the intensity of emotions. Elena spoke about how she used to create diversions, for example by changing jobs or relationships: "Anything for a distraction rather than deal with how I felt. Now that it's okay to feel how I feel, I have no need to create a distraction." Helen talked about using this strategy within the interview itself: "When it comes to describing something from a distance, it's fine. When the emotions start catching up with what I'm describing, then that's when I have to change the subject." In one other example, Janet was worried about an upcoming family gathering and commented, "It's going to be hard, but I'll have the kids there and they'll be a good distraction."

As we have suggested with other strategies for the management of feelings, when a woman consciously and deliberately chooses diversionary tactics as a way to cope in a particular situation, such maneuvers can be helpful. When the decision is unconscious, diversionary tactics may not always serve the adult survivor's interests. As with all such methods, it is helpful for therapists to appreciate and acknowledge to clients the resiliency implicit in such techniques when they were used before other alternatives were available. Certainly they are preferable to the survivor's having been overwhelmed by her feelings.

Humor

We anticipated much greater use of humor, perhaps because the first person we interviewed, Anne, relied on it so heavily in childhood and later, but only two other participants described it as an adult tactic. Anne told us often about the necessity of being able to laugh about bad things in order to survive. We have quoted Anne on the centrality of humor to preserve her sanity. Elena appreciated the humor in an Ellen Bass workshop in which she participated: "You didn't have to worry about would somebody understand or would somebody be offended or would they be skittish or would they get it. The jokes were pathetically sick, but where else could you tell a joke about what had happened to you?" Like Anne and her siblings, Galen and her brother "used to say . . . you got to laugh or you'll commit suicide, you know, like you've got to joke about things."

When humor is used in a way that acknowledges the horrors of abuse rather than denies them, it is a valuable resource. At times clients employ humor in a way that seems to simultaneously respect and deny the harsh reality of their history, and it can be complicated for therapists to figure out how much to appreciate it and how much to point out its avoidant function.

Spirituality

A number of our participants talked about the way religion or spirituality helped them manage their emotions. For example, Elena said, "It was a night when I was feeling particularly lonely and afraid, afraid to open my heart up again, afraid to be hurt. So it was one of those nights making a deal with God, 'If you'll help me not to be afraid and open my heart,' this was a Friday, 'I'll go to [Jewish] services Saturday morning.' And I felt like my heart had let go and opened up. And I went to services and felt very safe and very comfortable and very glad I was there."

When Felicia was asked about the most important relationship in her life, she responded: "I know this will sound strange. . . . It's not a person. When I have the conversion reaction sometimes, it's like I float off into another space somewhere. And when I go there, it's very calming and peaceful. And it's almost, I don't have to talk, but I had an understanding that I'm going to be okay and things of that nature. It's sort of like a sixth sense almost, because I know when danger is around, and that certain feeling comes. I guess maybe it's a relationship with something spiritual."

She told us this in the initial interviews, and at that time we struggled with whether to regard this as a religious experience. By the time of the follow-up interview, it was unequivocally clear that it was spiritual, in relationship to her view of God, and that it was helpful to her.

Spirituality was a major resource for our participants, partly in managing feelings, as we discuss here, and even more in helping them make sense of their traumatic histories, as we discuss later. Therapists need to take this aspect of their clients' resiliency seriously because it is an important strength in their survival and growth.

CLINICAL IMPLICATIONS

One finding particularly intrigued us, and it has clinical implications for therapists: *for these women, more strategies were not necessarily better*. Although we did not formally measure emotional adjustment, our impression was that the women who reported using the broadest range of techniques in both childhood and adulthood were not necessarily the best at effectively regulating their feelings. However, relying on just one or two strategies could sometimes be a handicap. For example, Helen reported using acting out (often self-destructively) as her only means of regulating her feelings in childhood. Clearly, this limited repertoire left her vulnerable to being overwhelmed by her emotions and also exposed her to potential harm from her acting out. However, Helen also came from what was in many ways the most abusive background with the fewest resources. This example best illustrates the need for therapists to bear in mind the *context* from which survivors came when judging their coping skills and adaptation. It is not a negative reflection on Helen's resiliency that she appeared to use only one defensive tactic in childhood; it is a reflection of the paucity of resources available to her in that world. For some other victim of abuse, with more supports in childhood, using only one technique to manage feelings might well reflect limited resiliency, and her therapist should keep that in mind when getting an overall picture of her strengths and vulnerabilities.

With adults, as we saw with these women in childhood, most of their coping strategies left them more or less aware of their emotions. Expressing or experiencing the feeling directly, getting help from others, having the feeling but hiding it from others, and self-soothing all left participants in touch with their feelings. In contrast, distancing from the feeling (numbing, shutting down, and so forth), somatizing, and some forms of acting out involved not being aware of the emotions. We suggest that therapists might fruitfully keep this in mind as they explore ways their clients can manage feelings. Having conscious access to feelings always gives more control and more choice.

In adulthood, participants' most common strategies included cognitive coping and experiencing or expressing. These strategies are quite different from the most common childhood technique— acting on feelings. As our participants gained cognitive capacity and created safer living environments, these more adaptive methods could flourish. These women were learning to value their feelings, tolerate their experiences, and express themselves more authentically. They took great pride in these developing abilities, in part because that added to their sense of integration. Therapists need to acknowledge the importance of this shift and teach clients ways to continue to develop in these directions. However, therapists also need to understand that even adult women who are resilient in many ways often rely on being able to get away from their feelings at times by such methods as behavioral coping and distancing or numbing.

Managing one's emotional life is crucial to adaptation and growth. The idea of managing feelings has been addressed by writers like Daniel Goleman in his important book, *Emotional Intelligence* (1996), and is regarded as one of the foundations of psychological health. In the face of extraordinary stress and distress, these women learned impressive techniques for managing intense and difficult feelings so that they could continue to function, and sometimes thrive, in many areas of their lives. Therapists can assist clients' healing by appreciating the strengths they show in this area of psychological functioning, helping them understand the context that both limited and supported the methods they developed, and helping them make conscious decisions about what works best for them in their current lives.

9

The Importance of Self-Care

Individuals who were abused by their families in childhood sometimes grow up with marked limitations in their ability to take care of themselves. Thus an important component of resiliency is self-care, and recovery is marked by an increasing ability to care for oneself effectively. Our participants' resiliency was apparent in the ways that many were able to take care of themselves, sometimes even in childhood or adolescence, often before beginning the formal process of recovery.

In some ways almost everything people do that is good for them can be seen as self-care. We have chosen to focus on a few salient dimensions, including how our participants set appropriate boundaries, soothed themselves, stopped self-abuse and other addictions, took care of their physical and emotional health, and used their leisure time. (Other important components of self-care are the strategies they developed to manage feelings, which were explored in the previous chapter.) Throughout, we emphasize the implications of this information for therapists.

SETTING BOUNDARIES

One of the most important aspects of self-care is learning to set appropriate boundaries. In women who have been traumatized and have had their physical and emotional boundaries violated repeatedly, learning to set boundaries is a crucial and challenging psychological and interpersonal task. Boundaries in physical, emotional, and relational arenas are not mutually exclusive; they overlap. Protecting physical boundaries involves setting limits around bodily contact, especially in sexual situations, and learning how to protect personal space. The most elemental aspect of physical boundaries is protection from further abuse.

In adolescence both Darlene and Felicia were driven to find ways to protect themselves physically. Darlene described the last time her brother physically abused her, when she was a young adolescent: "For some reason, he let me go, and on the wall next to our stove, we had one of those knife racks. So I grabbed a knife and I said, 'If you ever touch me again, I'm going to kill you.'"

Similarly, Felicia remembered a time when she was about fourteen, when she would not continue to be beaten by her mother. "I was much bigger then and I wasn't going to hit her, but I gave her a look. And I think she knew that I would hit her back if she hit me this time. That's the last time she ever tried to beat me. And I said, 'I'm going to do [what she had said to do]. I just want to finish this.' And then she went lunging at me, and I did like this and looked, and I had my hands in a fist. I remember catching myself, because I never want to hit my mother, but I just wasn't going to let her hit me."

It is unusual for a traumatized child, even an adolescent, to try to fend off an attacker physically. Therapists who hear such stories from a client should work with the woman to fully explore what such an event meant to her. These are often turning points in a survivor's sense of helplessness versus efficacy in defending her boundaries, physical and otherwise. Several important issues must be understood. First, why did she defend herself then? What pushed her too far or allowed her to try to defend herself? Second, how did she feel afterward? Did she feel powerful, as though she had regained control of her physical safety and therefore emotional dignity? Any range of feelings is likely to include guilt, rage, or shame at not having done it sooner. It is important to understand the impact her actions had on her environment as well as on her sense of herself. Therapists need to help clients appreciate how remarkable it is that they attempted any self-defense at all, given a history of abuse, and help them acknowledge the strength they still carry with them that allowed them to do that. These are the stories that shift the survivor's sense of herself from victim to survivor. For that reason they should be highlighted.

Several participants focused on learning to protect themselves physically as adults. For example, Galen told us, "I took a little bit of self-defense stuff for lesbians and gays. I also carry a kitty protector, which is on my keys, which has these two sharp things coming out. I can carry [it] in my pocket, but if someone tried to attack me, I would go like this and get their eyes."

Finding ways to protect themselves reflects resiliency. The women gained confidence that they could take care of themselves and had the tools to do it well if the need arose. Therapists should encourage any effort a client makes to increase her physical capability and knowledge of self-defense. Feeling physically strong helps her feel that she can defend her boundaries, and being stronger and trained in self-defense makes it more likely that she actually can. This increases her actual safety as well as her sense of safety in the world and decreases feelings of helplessness, freeing up emotional energy for other healing work.

For most of the women, geographical distance from former perpetrators, including family members, was necessary to give them a sense of protected space. (The resilient individuals described by Wolin and Wolin [1993] also made sure they had geographical distance from their dysfunctional and often abusive families.) For several, as we have said, college was a time of finding physical distance and making a break.

In later adolescence, Galen often thought about getting out of her hometown. "I was just feeling very trapped, and I was very poor, and I didn't think that I would ever be able to get out. Yet every day, the only thing that kept me alive was thinking that I would be able to get out sometime. So when I finally found college, and I went back to school that fall, [that] was what saved me, I think, from who knows what would happen."

Good physical boundaries also include protecting noncontact personal space. Anne was the participant who talked most explicitly about protecting her personal space in adulthood, probably because her mother routinely intruded on the physical space of her adult children. One of our favorites is Anne's description of learning to say no to her mother—a formidable woman whom almost nobody attempted to thwart. They were in her parents' house. Not long before, her sister had let her parents know that she had just gotten married without telling them. For a very long time, their mother remained bitter and disappointed and kept recounting her distress:

> This story came up all the time when my mother was drinking. All the time. Just say the right word, press the button, the whole tape. There was no interrupting the tape. . . . And I turned to her at one point, sitting at the dining room table, and I said, "Mother, I know you're disappointed. I know you're not happy about this. I don't want to hear about it any more." And she threw a New York phone book at me. Missed. Stormed out [laughs]. Slammed the door. And didn't speak to me for three months [laughs]. Didn't invite me for Thanksgiving. I was not invited for Thanksgiving. But it was worth it.

In the course of her therapy and development, Anne learned to say no to her mother in a variety of ways. When therapists broaden the idea of physical boundaries to include personal space, they give clients much-needed permission to be more assertive and self-protective around this issue. Women survivors often need help focusing on when and where they need more distance and space for themselves. In our clinical experience, many traumatized women lack appropriate entitlement. The clinician should work with the client on increasing awareness of her own needs and her ability and right to assert those needs effectively. Furthermore, boundaries with the family of origin are often the most difficult to build, maintain, and negotiate. Success in other domains often serves to inform a survivor about how she might do it more successfully with her family.

Maintaining emotional boundaries entails protecting one's feelings and the right to experience and express those feelings. It includes forbidding other people to say or do things that create hurtful feelings and thus safeguarding an emotionally healthy environment. Ilona had focused on developing her belief in her right to express her feelings. She spoke for many survivors, as well as many other women, when she commented on how hard it was for her to assert herself and her feelings: "That's another thing about feeling. You can't say you're uncomfortable until you find your voice and can say, 'This is unacceptable.' There are still situations that come up in my life that I find it very difficult to say, 'This is unacceptable.' For me, it would be just as easy to blend into the woodwork."

With help, clients can learn to be proactive in their self-care by anticipating issues. This kind of anticipation is crucial to setting and maintaining emotional boundaries. Clinicians can work with women in therapy to reflect on situations that have felt uncomfortable and to learn from these situations in order to anticipate future needs for regulating emotional boundaries. Typically a traumatized woman is not aware of her discomfort until she is in the middle of a situation, or sometimes after it is over. Then she feels helpless to change it. Over time, with the help of the therapist, she can gradually learn to recognize her feelings in the moment and, eventually, to anticipate those feelings.

Our examples reflect our participants' knowledge, sometimes born of long years of therapy, that they needed to protect their emotional boundaries. The fact that few of their narratives described setting boundaries during childhood may mean that children are not able to do this or that it's not safe to assert one's emotional boundaries under violent circumstances. It is more likely that it happens in childhood in subtle ways that are not accessible to conscious awareness and thus cannot be remembered afterward.

Finding the right distance between two people is the heart of relational boundaries. Many survivors become too involved with friends or intimate partners for their own or others' comfort, whereas others, in an effort to protect themselves, remain too distant to get much satisfaction. Thus, developing a sense of a membrane between oneself and another that is the right thickness—not too porous, not too thick—is a challenge for many survivors. Because all of these women's early relationships involved serious abuse, learning to set appropriate relational boundaries with their families was a momentous task.

Beth described differences she experienced in her recent intimate relationships, compared with earlier ones, and her sense of boundaries: "There's a real quality of difference in the relationships that I've had. I feel much more myself and like I have boundaries, and that those boundaries are respected. One of the big issues between me and the guy I just broke up with is that I think he had this feeling of being very driven to be with me. I mean he wanted to be with me all the time, and I have a life, . . . and I had to set real limits. It used to be like that. I think that's a mark of my recovery that it's not that way anymore."

Anne told us: "I thought I had to share; I thought I had to tell, I had to expose, and it's taken me a long time to realize that I don't have to do that. I don't have to always be vulnerable."

Another dimension of boundaries that emerged from the women's narratives was the difference between a woman's protecting herself physically, emotionally, and relationally from an intrusion or an attack and proactively asserting her needs. For example, Beth told us about the guidelines she has established with her ex-husband in order feel safe in their interactions involving their son.

"I set very clear boundaries with him, and one of the things I don't discuss with him is his life or my life. I discuss [our son and our son's] issues."

In a powerful example, as a nine- or ten-year-old child, Felicia was proactive when she confronted her father:

> My father and mother had some tension, and I told my Dad one time, I said, "Dad, you know, I know you and Mom love each other, but you're probably not made for each other, to live together. There's a lot of tension, and I don't like it. So why don't you just leave? Just go ahead and leave and do what you want with your life." He looked at me and he says, "That's between me and your mother to take care of." But what I was trying to tell him though is I was feeling the tension too.

Proactively stating one's needs means trying to change the situation or set the conditions so that the environment is safe and there will be less need to protect oneself later.

Setting boundaries both proactively and reactively is crucial to development. Some participants could do one but not the other. By the time of the initial interviews most had developed the skill of protecting themselves physically from unwanted contact; by the follow-up interviews all had learned to do this within reasonable limits. However, at the initial interviews most were still working on these skills in the emotional and relational domains and were developing the ability to speak up for their needs when they were not necessarily having to defend themselves.

With the help of skilled therapists, women can observe how they set boundaries—proactively or reactively—and increase their awareness of what they need to do to protect themselves more effectively. Clinicians might similarly expect their female clients to work longer at developing these skills in the emotional and relational domains. Even small successes should be highlighted wherever possible as an example of the client's resilience that should be nurtured and cultivated.

COPING IN CHILDHOOD AND ADULTHOOD

Our participants told us about a number of ways they soothed themselves in childhood. Elena found small places where she could go and feel safe:

> I found every small safe place I could create. In the living room before my parents took down this wall, the front door had an entry hall. And then there was this half wall that had a planter at the top and it created a corner into the living room, and there was a big oversized chair in that corner and a heating vent. And I used to sit in that space. And early mornings when nobody was up, that's where I would be. I'd read there.

When asked what it was like to be in a small space, she said, "Safe. People couldn't get at me; people couldn't bother me. I could control the space. I was a short, small kid. And so every space was too big for me. I always felt overwhelmed, so I kept trying to find these little safe spaces. And I tried to be invisible as much as I could."

In addition to writing poetry, Felicia listened to the Nina Simone records of her older sister. Janet had some rituals that she was embarrassed to tell us (although we think they are common among survivors and in fact help them get through), that involved counting squares of toilet paper, or counting bathroom tiles. She said the counting was soothing to her and helped her get away from her emotional pain and turmoil.

We suspect that abused children, resilient and otherwise, comfort themselves in other ways but are unaware of their methods when they use them or have no memory of them later. In either case they would not be able to describe them retrospectively. Our participants were much more aware and focused on the ways they soothed and supported themselves in adulthood, partly because it was being emphasized in therapy. They had all learned that they needed to focus carefully on taking care of themselves, and many emphasized that they rely on themselves for that, no matter how many other people are in their lives to help.

Carrie described how she was getting through the pain of the recovery process. She said, "You need to reach back to that time when you felt cared about or loved." At another time she told us, "You need the healthy parts of yourself to help the parts of yourself that are hurt." She described how she coped with being stirred up and uncomfortable following Thanksgiving with the family: "I was feeling lousy [laughs]. So I was hurting and then finally found this kind of image [remembering the sheets my grandmother put on my bed, which made me feel special as a child] to be able to kind of just cry and feel sad." Finding a supportive and nurturing image gave her the strength to allow herself to feel her sadness, and when she did that, she felt more whole.

In adulthood the participants have had more ways to do things to make themselves feel better than they did as children. For example, Anne told us about visiting her mother: "I always felt like I had to drive her car, because I would feel like I wasn't an adult, and if I drove a car I could remember that I must be an adult because I know how to drive a car [laughs]. It was something about driving her car and maybe also going out by myself away from her house that I had some little measure of control over the whole thing, because I felt so, so small."

Part of adult emotional self-care is recognizing what one has been through and giving oneself credit. As Helen put it, "I take care of myself more. I have respect for myself more. I don't like saying good stuff about myself, but I know that I've made it through a war. I got to be strong for that, a pat on the back every now and then." Therapy is a place for women survivors to construct a story—their story—about how they have survived. That story is important to put into words, particularly in the presence of another, the therapist. It is a story that will gradually change in subtle ways throughout a woman's recovery and beyond. Each woman's story of how she takes care of herself, soothes herself, is important and valid in the context of her experiences. The therapist can work to help frame the story through the lens of resilience.

Even self-destructive methods of self-soothing imply some attempt to take care of the self, however misguided the effort. But these methods often increase the survivor's shame. Every symptom or maladaptive behavior is there for a reason, usually a reason that protects some part of the self, even as it causes harm to another part. Therapists can help clients ward off shame by reframing behaviors in terms of the purpose they have served. Those insights can then be used to establish more adaptive, more broadly self-caring behaviors to soothe painful feelings.

STOPPING SELF-ABUSE AND ADDICTION

In listening to our participants talk about their recovery process and how they learned self-care, we could see that, for several of them, one important component in the process was recovery from self-abuse and addiction. We agree with others in the field that addictive behavior includes a much larger class of events than simply substance abuse. Self-abusive behaviors, substance abuse, and the abuse of food are all characterized by the compulsive use of various kinds of substances or behaviors that are designed to alter feeling states. Thus the process of recovery from the misuse of drugs and alcohol is part of a larger process of recovery from self-abusive behavior that includes eating disorders and promiscuity. Galen and Helen were addicted to alcohol and involved in other self-abusive behaviors. Listening to their thoughts about the process of stopping self-abuse and addiction gave us insight into their resiliency.

Stages of Stopping Self-Abuse and Addiction

As our participants described their growing ability to stop self-abuse and addictions, we saw different stages of that process. For both Galen and Helen, recovery from compulsions involved coming to understand the relationship between their history of trauma and substance abuse and their other self-abusive behaviors. Galen stopped drinking and stopped her promiscuous sexual behavior at the same time and understood the link between them perfectly. Helen, like Galen, had also been sober for about four years at the time of the initial interviews and talked about alcohol abuse in rela-tion to her trauma history. Describing a period in her life when she was drinking heavily and engaged in promiscuous behavior, she stated, "Then I realized I was a survivor of sexual abuse. And I just realized, this is why I'm involved with these crazy people. And I finally ended up being able to get away." Similar to the way Galen connected drinking and promiscuity, Helen associated drinking with self-abuse. She told us she used cutting as an alternative to drink-ing to manage her feelings. She said, "At that point (after being triggered by an anniversary reaction to the cult abuse), I was hav-ing a hard time and cutting myself, and I wanted to not cut myself, so I went [to a respite care facility]. I wanted not to drink." She also said about stopping cutting: "I didn't know what it was about. Now I do."

In a graphic illustration of the link between her addictive behav-iors, Helen went through a bulimic episode during her first year of sobriety. "Right about last year, the cutting ended, the food thing went into last summer. The cutting stopped last year. The smoking started once I ended the relationship. Now I'm trying not to smoke, but I'm smoking. I have a patch, but I still smoke with the patch on. I'm wondering what the next in line, what the next addiction will be."

Later she added, "I like to spend, too. That's another one of my addictions. I got myself $13,000 in debt on credit cards. I'm still paying them off. I've got them down to five now." Impressively, five years later by the time of the follow-up interview, she had paid off her debts and was much more in control of her spending.

So for several of our participants self-abuse and addictive behaviors were closely linked. Therapists working with survivors at an early stage of their recovery, when many struggle with these issues, need to be mindful of the way these different problematic behaviors tend to substitute for one another. It helps a client to know that she may be vulnerable to starting a new one, or finding herself reverting to an old one, when she stops or greatly reduces an ongoing addiction.

Increases in Feelings and Memories After Stopping Addictions

For both Galen and Helen, stopping drinking and other self-abusive behaviors was associated with increased feelings about, and intrusive memories of, their abuse histories. Galen's response to the difficulties was to write. She said, "So I started to feel a lot of things and I just really mourned, I started to mourn. Well, actually I wrote, and I wrote a poem that was about the abuse and about the loss of my Dad's life, the loss of my Mom's, and how I want to be free." In response to that sense of loss, she said, she cried, smoked cigarettes, and started seeing a therapist. Then when she went back to school and was out of the supportive and healthier environment, she began drinking again. She commented, "I think I was trying to numb that out, the feeling of loss." Similarly, smoking helped Galen numb her feelings about the abuse. Stopping smoking brought back both memories and feelings about the abuse.

For Helen too, sobriety was associated with an increase in feelings about and memories of the abuse. She talked about the connection between sobriety and recovering memories of her abusive childhood: "The memories started coming up at four and one-half months sober; and then like eight months sober is when I realized it was my father who sexually abused me." After a year of sobriety she remembered a history of satanic abuse within her family and was able to remain sober by making use of occasional brief voluntary hospitalization and "lots of [AA] meetings." Helen described how sobriety is still hard sometimes, "especially when memories are coming up, but it gets easier, then it passes."

Therapists need to help clients understand that one function of destructive addictive behaviors is to ward off painful feelings. When they begin to move away from these behaviors, the strong feelings and memories often come back. At that point, therapists should help clients use all of the skills and resources they have been developing to safely contain and process these traumatic experiences.

Stopping Self-Abuse as the Beginning of Recovery

Both Galen and Helen began their process of recovery from trauma with stopping addiction and self-abuse. Both developed clarity about these addictive behaviors and how they related to their history of abuse. Once they achieved this awareness, they determined to stop both the addictive and self-abusive behaviors. For both, having a cognitive framework, in this case a way of understanding the addictive behaviors, was enormously helpful in changing them.

Galen's process of recovery from addictions began when she found herself in a healthy work environment in which people were not abusing substances and were honoring their feelings. Clearly, her decision to work in this context was a resilient one and a step toward becoming sober, whether she was aware of that at the time or not. Repeatedly through these interviews we have seen resiliency represented by an individual's decision to enter a particular context (school, work, and so forth) that later becomes central to their recovery. At the time they couldn't say why they were making that choice; their reasons for making the decision were not conscious ones.

Similarly, Helen began recovery when she started to associate with a woman who was moving away from addiction. She stated,

"And I started seeing another woman, who was in recovery from alcoholism. She was drinking at the time, but she was in recovery a little bit." Like Galen's, Helen's recoveries from her history of sexual abuse and from addiction began together. As we have said, Helen's mother was an alcoholic, and when she died, Helen started going to Al-Anon meetings, not aware that she herself was alcoholic. She then decided she wanted to stop drinking. At that time, however, her friends and associates all drank, so she thought maybe she would give up beer but still be able to enjoy a rum cake with her friends. A month later she drank Irish coffee with her family at Thanksgiving and then on New Years' Eve, and then decided she needed to stop altogether; she began her abstinence with a month-long inpatient detoxification program and has been abstinent since.

When we asked Helen about insights that kept her going in this process, she gave a wonderfully resilient response that reveals the inner resources that can develop during recovery from trauma:

> Just that I'm OK and that whatever happens, I'm going to be OK. I just thought about that coming in here . . . especially at the beginning when getting sober, when I would be distressed, I thought that the feeling was never going to end, that I would feel this way forever. And I feel like I've learned that, no matter how bad I feel, that feeling is going to pass. And that other feelings are going to come in too, like that I'm going to feel joy, I'm going to feel faith, I'm going to feel hope, the feelings change, and I think that really, really keeps me going.

The stories we heard reveal the role of addiction in protecting the survivor from feelings. The feelings associated with abuse are experienced as emotionally threatening, so much so that the survivor is willing to hurt herself in other ways in order to defend herself against these feelings. In therapy, gradually increasing tolerance for feelings and experiencing those feelings within the safety of a trusting relationship is a significant part of recovery from addictions. At the same time, addictions act as a hiding place for feelings that should be dealt with in therapy. Therefore therapists are advised to keep the issue of addiction on the table as needing to be addressed before other recovery work can safely continue. It is important for many clients that they make a commitment to sobriety or abstinence from the addictive behavior and establish some level of abstinence before other work around feelings is attempted. Slowly building the client's capacity to tolerate distressing emotions is central to making it possible for her to give up an addiction and also begins to prepare her for the intense emotions she will feel when she stops the addictive behavior.

PHYSICAL SELF-CARE

Many of the women talked about learning to take care of their bodies, which is essential to self-care. Several told us they worked out regularly and viewed that as essential to their mental health. Beth was particularly clear about the role of exercise in her emotional well-being. As we have described, she told us of an incident in which she was feeling very sad and upset after leaving her son at the airport to return to his father's home, and then noticed she was getting a headache, which she understood was about "not dealing with the sadness or the pain." So she went off to her health club and worked out for a short time. She said, "Even that made me feel better and helped me get back into my body. I was sad, of course, but it helped me feel like I was a whole person again."

Several participants talked about learning either to limit their use of drugs or to stop altogether as part of their developing self-care. Janet said that at one point she had been smoking marijuana and had a bad experience, so she simply decided not to smoke anymore and did not. Beth learned that stimulants affected her more than most people, she thought because of her history of abuse, so she greatly limited her intake of caffeine and alcohol.

In an example of a different kind of physical self-care, Galen told us about telling her gynecologist that she didn't like the way the physician hurt her during the pelvic examination. When the doctor said it shouldn't hurt, Galen said she told her, "I'm a survivor of sexual abuse, OK? And this is like scary for me."

Felicia noticed the morning of one of the interviews that her body was jerking, as it tended to do when she became more manic. She told us she said to herself, "Just slow down the pace a little, so that your body can get some rest." In this case, she was attending to her body, which then allowed her to know what she needed to do to take care of herself.

These women demonstrated considerable resilience in attending to their physical needs. This is typically not an easy task for survivors because they often grow up in families that, in a variety of direct and indirect ways, teach them that their physical feelings and needs are not important and that it is selfish of them to want to attend to them. Care of the body (what one participant termed "the battle-ground") is thus an emotionally laden task for a survivor of physical and sexual abuse. It is, however, something that needs to be attended to and encouraged in therapy.

LEISURE

All of our participants were aware of the need to spend relaxing and enjoyable time, leisure time, particularly when they were in an intense process of recovery from trauma. Several described the importance of getting away from the intensity and the focus on their histories and just having fun. Some were able to do that; for many, there were external obstacles to enjoying leisure time—usually too little time or money. A number of our participants also described inner obstacles to taking time for relaxation and pleasure. Ilona told us it took a while to learn to enjoy leisure without feeling guilty. At the time of the follow-up interview, Darlene told us she was enjoying her leisure time; she loved doing such things as going to the

African Art Museum at the Smithsonian Institute. But she was aware of some inner constraints on what she could allow herself to do. "It's funny. My leisure stuff is all still somehow learning-related, only every once in a while I do stuff that is pure goofiness." She looked forward to a time when she could enjoy pure goofiness, without needing always to be learning something or developing herself.

A few were in an earlier phase of their struggle to have fun. In the initial interviews Elena talked about what she noticed about herself: "I just noticed that my habitual response is to go watch TV, and then I noticed that I don't want to. So that's still what I go to do, but then I think, 'Well, no, I don't want to do that.' So it's still happening." She was perfectly clear she wanted that to change and could see that it was beginning to change. At the time of the first interviews, she told us she sometimes would come home exhausted after work, "and sometimes I can do nothing but watch TV or sit and listen to music but I'm not retreating from myself or the world in the way that I used to." By the time of the follow-up, she and her partner had evolved many satisfying and rich ways to spend their leisure time.

Felicia struggled constantly to achieve a better balance between work and play; she knew she was still working too much. However, she had one powerful moment that let her know how important leisure activities were to her. She had gone to Maine and climbed Cadillac Mountain: "It started to get real cloudy. And the clouds started to come in real heavy, and I was sitting there, and all of a sudden, it looked like you were walking in the clouds! At that moment I realized I was glad I was alive. And I said, 'I want to get more enjoyment out of life. And things are going to get better.' That was a very powerful moment for me."

These women's ability to enjoy leisure was, for many of them, a work in progress. Carrie seemed to surprise herself when she told us during the initial interviews, "I've probably had more fun in the past—this is awful to say because there's kind of this undercurrent of pain or sadness, but I've really probably had more fun in the past year. . . . I've just been a little more footloose and fancy free, I guess you could say."

In therapy, the focus is so often on pain and relief that room is not always made for attention to fun. We believe that the therapist can subtly encourage more space in the client's life for pleasure by making space for it in therapy. This may allow a later shift from surviving to living, which is after all a major goal of psychotherapy.

10

Making Sense of the Abuse

It is in our nature as human beings to try to make sense of our experience. In fact, a normal part of development is the increasing need and ability to construct a personal narrative that gives a sense of purpose and meaning to our lives. When something bad happens to us, we want to know why. We try to find a reason for it. And most of us have tried to understand the bad things that happen to other people—the victims of war, violent crime, natural disasters, famine, and abuse.

Trauma survivors face the even greater difficulty of having to try to integrate awful, painful, damaging, and seemingly meaningless experiences into their life narratives. A traumatic event is something that is so outside the realm of normal experience that it does not fit into a person's existing framework of understanding about the world. It can either destroy the sense of meaning a person constructed before the abuse, or the event must be pushed out of awareness if it cannot be integrated into any existing framework of meaning.

However, terrible life events sometimes have positive effects. Two researchers, Martha Burt and Bonnie Katz (1987), found in their study of women who had been raped that some women reported having been changed in important and positive ways by the experience. The positive changes they reported included knowing themselves better, knowing who their real friends were, feeling that life had more meaning, becoming more aware of such social issues as violence toward women, and becoming involved in social action. Individuals who have been abused as children have an even greater challenge in this regard because they grow up experiencing the world as a painful and dangerous place. For them, like the women in our sample, meaning making involves not only trying to make sense of their suffering but constructing an alternative view of the world in which this suffering is not the dominant feature. These women must integrate the horrific things that have happened to them with the hope that they can have a better future.

In listening to our participants, we were struck by how their ways of making meaning changed over time, as they moved from childhood to adulthood and then through their recovery process. We will highlight these shifts as we go along.

We begin this chapter by focusing on how our participants made meaning of their abuse in childhood, which was predominantly by blaming themselves for it. We then describe how this view shifted from childhood to adulthood and explore why the shift occurred. The next shift we focus on is how some of the participants began to see the abuse as occurring within "a larger organization of things," to use Felicia's words. We then move, with our participants, beyond their struggle to know why the abuse occurred; we examine ways they make meaning in their current lives through religion, altruism, and work.

SELF-BLAME

Many of the women we interviewed talked about a time when they blamed themselves for the abuse perpetrated against them. This is a very common feeling in childhood victims. Although in the long-term self-blame can be damaging, researchers Silver, Boon, and Stone (1983), among others, have found that it can serve an important function in childhood for many abuse survivors. One positive aspect of self-blame is that it allows a child to feel more in control of the abuse. If a child thinks, "Daddy does those things to me because

I'm bad," the child can preserve the hope that if she is good enough the violations will stop. However, if circumstances do not get better, as they generally don't because the child's behavior usually has little or nothing to do with the abuse, the child must conclude that she is bad—a view that is both inaccurate and destructive to the child. Another positive aspect of self-blame, suggested by Feinauer and Stuart (1996), is that it allows the abused child to maintain a positive attachment to the abusive parent. This enables the child to avoid blaming the parent, which would not be tolerated in many abusive families, and thus to survive; she depends on her family for everything she needs to live. Thus, blaming oneself can be viewed in the short term as a resilient strategy with potential negative long-term consequences.

Because self-blame has been spoken about so often as a way for children to make sense of abuse, we were not surprised to find self-blame described by a number of our participants. Elena described her struggle:

> It wasn't me, and that it just wasn't me, and it wasn't me. That's a hard one to let go, because in that most fundamental soul, there's that doubt. You know, how could anyone do this unless I had done something to deserve it is beyond my imagination. That without that cause someone could have done it. . . . So it took a while to let that go. And I would let it go for a year. And then it would come back in some other moment of anguish reliving the past. Just that absolute inability to believe that someone would choose to do that to a little kid without cause.

For some, like Janet, self-blame involved internalizing a pervasive sense of badness. "I internalized it then, and I did think that I was just bad. I constantly felt like I must be a disappointment to my parents, like too bad they got a kid like me, like, they must be so embarrassed of me. So I constantly felt like it was something, I did feel like it was about me, instead of about them. Because they just were so respected in the community. So how could it be them; they must have gotten this ugly, horrible kid."

Janet's words capture the destructive nature of self-blame. As a child she could only assume that she was the problem, leaving her feeling like "this ugly, horrible kid." Only in adulthood, as we discuss later, did she begin to realize that her parents had their own issues and problems that accounted for their treatment of her.

Carrie was not aware of feeling that she was bad. As she described it, "Initially, before I started to remember [the abuse], somewhere like I was always, without really being aware of this, but defending against a sense of myself as being bad. . . . It was locked away, all these feelings locked away, just this fear that I was, even though I tried really hard to be a good person, that I was really bad."

Elena spoke about how blaming herself actually helped her cope emotionally in childhood:

> I also didn't feel like I had done anything wrong when it came down to it; I really didn't. It was just the reason I had used to live in order to survive. [Interviewer: It sounds like blaming yourself gave you some sense of strength.] Well it allowed me to keep living in the world, because if I really accepted the notion that adults were capriciously cruel, then I wouldn't be out in the world, because I'd never know who or where the next attack will come from. And I don't think I knew that at the time, but I think that's true. So as long as I was responsible, I had some control over my life, then I was responsible for what happened to me and I could keep functioning at some level in the world.

From Elena's words, we understand that she needed to believe at some level that she had some control over what happened to her.

We also see that from her perspective this distortion played a useful role in enhancing her resilience, allowing her to go on in the world. In fact, according to Feinauer and Stuart (1996), for adults dealing with such traumatic experiences as rape, self-blame can be an adaptive strategy.

Not all participants accepted responsibility for the abuse they suffered in childhood. Galen told us that she worked very hard to hold on to a view of herself as good, and that was an important source of strength for her in childhood. We would add that it reflected her resiliency. She said, "I really tried to think of myself as real good or that I really could like myself. That somehow even though all the stuff was gross and bad, maybe I am really good."

Overall then, among the women we spoke with, most tended in childhood to blame themselves for the abuse. Most internalized some sense of themselves as bad. Elena gave voice to the issue of maintaining an illusion of control by blaming herself. This is something we suspect applies to many of these women, although they did not put words to it. Clinicians often see survivors of a traumatic experience believing that in some way they should have been able to control it. For Carrie it was the belief that if only she were good, things would be better for her. This is a child's way of maintaining a belief in a just world, a predictable world. This says something about how important that perspective is for people to maintain and how costly trauma is, either to a person's sense of self or sense of other (the world). One or the other is inevitably made "bad" in the process of making sense of why bad things happen.

Therapists need to assess whether self-blame is playing a more adaptive or more destructive role in a client's recovery. They should not move too quickly to reassure survivors of their blamelessness before discovering what it means to them. Ultimately, the most resilient and adaptive strategy for many may be understanding where they can have some reasonable impact and control over what happens to them. They should combine that understanding with reducing their blame and shame, understanding their innocence, and accepting some of what that innocence meant at the time of the abuse in terms of not having had power or control. Therapists can support this kind of resilience by helping clients develop their ability to discriminate between situations where they can and cannot effect change. This includes challenging a client's initial perceptions of helplessness and helping them see ways they can take effective action. In situations that are entirely out of a client's control, therapists can offer validation and support in accepting such a situation or take some action that may not change circumstances but may change a client's experience of things (for example, focus on self-care strategies, issues of self-forgiveness, and self-love).

SHIFTING BLAME FROM SELF TO PERPETRATOR

All of the women who talked about their struggle with self-blame described consciously working on shifting the blame for the abuse from themselves to the perpetrator. This process did not begin until adulthood when the women were out of the abusive homes and no longer dependent on their parents. We wondered whether separation from an abusive family is a prerequisite for the process of shifting blame away from oneself. Therapists should consider this point when working with children who still live with their abusive family. And whether the child or the perpetrator has been removed from the home is important; both considerations may make a significant difference to the therapy. The degree of a client's separation, physical and psychological, from her family should also be considered when treating adults.

In the interviews, many of our participants addressed the issue of problems and blame residing with their perpetrators or caretakers (often the same people). Half suggested that these others may have had problematic histories, offering an explanation for why they were abusive. Anne said, "I think [the abuse] happened to me because my parents had unresolved problems from their families of origin. And we were just there. I don't think that it was God punishing me."

Felicia described it this way:

> The way I understand it now, there are a lot of people
> that aren't healthy in the world. And for various reasons
> they didn't get what they needed when they were young,
> or they have some quirk in their personality; they don't
> see the child as a human being, just as an object you tell
> what to do. And so they just think they can do whatever
> they want, and children and other people get hurt. And
> it's not because the child was bad. It's not even because
> the adult who might be a victim or something is bad.

In the words of these women, we can see the developmental process in their shifting frameworks of understanding. They seemed to be moving away from self-blame, although not so far away that the idea did not continue to arise. They could develop and believe these more sophisticated explanations only in adulthood.

Other participants offered more specific psychological interpretations about their abusers as part of their way of understanding why they had been abused. For example, Helen described the emotional abuse by her mother as occurring when her mother was in an "alter" or dissociative state: "The core of my mother, my real mother, was a wonderful woman. She was very caring, very nurturing, very, but she wasn't there that often either. She was behind the booze or the personalities, whatever." Ilona stated simply, "Why did it happen? It happened because I was living with a crazy person! [laughs] Pure and simple, it happened because this person couldn't take care of herself, let alone take care of a child."

Therapy played an important role in these women's ability to shift the way they made meaning of their abuse. In fact, helping survivors make this shift is an important role of therapy. Several participants described how their therapists had helped them move from blaming themselves to blaming the perpetrator. Often this involved strategies such as looking at a child the same age as they were when they were abused and asking themselves, "Is what happened to her that child's fault?"

This technique of helping a client gain perspective on her experience is often useful in helping survivors get a more realistic perspective on what happened and see that they were not to blame. This may be one reason group treatment is so helpful for trauma survivors—they get the benefit of many views of their experience that are more objective than their own. And it is often easier for a survivor to challenge another person's self-blame than her own. To give up self-blame often means giving up a sense of control but also allows a survivor to feel compassion for herself.

Shifting blame from oneself to the perpetrator is an aspect of making meaning that is essential to the process of recovery. Like the other components of the process—stopping self-abuse and addiction and accepting feelings—making this shift was, for our participants, an ongoing process. For example, Carrie talked in the initial interviews about where she was in the process of shifting blame from herself: "I'm just starting to get to a point where I can kind of grasp that at an adult level to the extent that I can feel compassion for myself rather than blame. I really just felt a lot of responsibility, and it's only been recently that I've been able to really feel how awful all this was for me—to be able to forgive myself, and have some compassion."

For some women, shifting away from self-blame also meant gaining a new understanding of why they had been in abusive relationships in adulthood. Galen and Ilona told us that once they understood the context of this behavior, they realized that they were not to blame for the repetition of abusive circumstances in their lives. Galen said:

> That was spring of '89 when I realized I was a survivor
> of sexual abuse as a child. At that time I was involved

with a woman who was very abusive to me, a woman who had raped me about six months prior to that time. And I put everything together, and I realized I wasn't to blame for what was going on with me, I wasn't crazy, that this is why, it's because my father treated me like a sex object. . . . And that's when I broke up with this woman. And that's when I chose sobriety and cleaned my slate up.

That realization, that clarity, allowed her to choose sobriety, to say no to the self-destructive pattern. Relinquishing self-blame allowed her to take positive action in her life.

These women's growing ability to shift from a self-focused and self-blaming perspective in childhood to a broader, more complex understanding of the psychological forces and motivations contributing to their own and others' behavior illustrates a developmental process that psychiatrist William Beardslee (1989) has described in nonabused individuals. It is a tribute to our participants' resiliency that many of them were able to make this shift and stop blaming themselves.

The work of psychotherapy with a survivor is often to help her make this shift by encouraging her to examine what happened to her from a different perspective (imagining another child at the same age as the client when abused, to elicit reality testing and compassion for herself). Clinicians can also support a client's involvement in group therapy, where she can gain some objectivity with regard to her experience. Ultimately, clients need to develop more complex narratives about themselves and others. Therapists can support this development by questioning the client's understanding of the influence on and motivation of others, in this way encouraging her to consider other answers to the question, Why did this happen? It is especially helpful for therapists, early in the process, to understand and acknowledge the role that self-blame likely served a client in childhood.

All people go through a developmental process of broadening one's view outward from the self, to others, to larger forces in the world. Trauma interrupts the normal course of this development. As psychologist Bertram Cohler has said (1991), the ability to continue to develop a broader perspective in the face of abuse is evidence of resilience, or it contributes to an individual's resilience.

THE BIG PICTURE

Several of these women in adulthood constructed a framework of understanding about their abuse that extended beyond themselves and other individuals to "a larger organization of things." For Felicia, this was a philosophical framework that she, remarkably, developed in childhood. She spoke about how her philosophical understanding helped her reframe her sense of self-blame:

> I did [blame myself] for a while, but [when I was nine] I read this book about general philosophies throughout the world. And they talked about all the different philosophies. And after I read that, I still blamed myself until now, but I did know in the back of my mind, things will happen. . . . When I read that book on philosophies, I was thinking to myself, "There is a bigger picture; we're all connected and things happen. And it doesn't always have to be the person's fault if they're a victim of something."

Felicia's philosophical understanding enabled her to begin to relinquish self-blame without completely relinquishing her sense of control in the world. She went on to say, "It's just that there's a larger organization of things going on in life. And we like to think we have control and we do to some degree. But there are other things that are greater than ourselves that are also operating. And oftentimes, something might happen to you and you say, 'Why?' And sometimes they're learning experiences, sometimes it's just meanness. But that's the order of the world, the way it is, and so bad things can happen."

This view realistically allows that bad things can happen to good people. Beginning as a young child, Felicia has been able over time to construct a view of the world that left her feeling realistically empowered to take care of herself but also allowed her to feel compassion for herself if she were hurt.

Galen found a sociological framework useful in understanding the context within which she was abused. "I think it's an epidemic of violence against women and children. And that's why it happened to me, because I was a child and then I was a woman [laughs]. And so I think it's because of misogyny, because of classism, because of homophobia. [Interviewer: It sounds like how you've come to understand it has been very helpful to you.] Yeah. Totally. That's always something that's really helped me is being able to put it in a larger picture, to understand it in a social context really helps me a lot."

For Galen, understanding her negative life experiences within a social context was helpful. Much of her understanding about the way the world works was organized around the injustices she saw perpetrated against people based on prejudice and power differentials. She appeared to be very identified with groups that had been persecuted in some way in our society, and she adopted or constructed a sociopolitical understanding about the suffering and abuse she had experienced and witnessed. She saw her own experiences as unfortunate but not surprising, given the sociological forces at work in our society. To her credit, she did not accept these forces as inevitable or immutable. Rather, her experience mobilized her desire to work against social injustice. Like Galen, Darlene also understood her experiences as occurring in a world where there is a significant degree of violence against women and found that framework helpful in the ways she made meaning of her history. Donna Howard (1996) has written about the importance of what she describes as "the role of the overarching ideology, such as afrocentricism or religious affiliations" (p. 258) in the resiliency of African Americans. Clearly these were strengths in Darlene, but the idea can be extended to anyone who has suffered adversity.

For several of the women we interviewed, finding a broader context within which to understand their experiences proved quite useful. It allowed them to broaden their view about why they were abused, countering feelings of self-blame and fostering more adaptive frameworks through which to understand their experience. It also allowed them to feel connected to others in the world and to take interest in or action toward helping them. Therapists can facilitate or support clients' efforts to develop a larger framework by listening for evidence of their sense of how the world works and encouraging deeper exploration of these views and beliefs. Often therapists can be helpful by offering a framework through their interpretations, such as a focus on the importance of a traditional feminine self or a focus on the role of power in relationships. Ultimately, however, each survivor needs to find a framework that makes sense to her, given her life experiences and cultural background. Whatever their own views, therapists must help clients develop perspectives that work for them. However, if a client's framework of understanding makes her feel powerless and the world seem all bad, thus giving her a sense of worthlessness or hopelessness, these views need to be examined, questioned, and challenged.

MOVING BEYOND WHY

Even though all of the women we spoke with struggled in different ways to make sense of why the abuse occurred, two spoke more directly to that struggle. They questioned the role, in their process of healing, of struggling to understand why the abuse happened. Darlene put it very well: "I think I used to spend more [time thinking about it]. When people directly ask me about it, I start to think about it more. But I don't think I'll ever know. And I think I've just reached a point where knowing why is not the important thing in me."

Similarly, Elena told us, "I think part of the reason I don't think about anymore, why did it happen. It's because there is no answer; there's no good answer. There's nothing productive that can come out of it. Because . . . I can only stay in bed for so long, and cry for so long, and whack beds for so long, and scream for so long. And then I've got to see that I have enough healing to go forward."

Silver, Boon, and Stone (1983) and others have written about the fact that, even though a survivor may feel the need to answer the question of why the abuse occurred, answering it is not as important as trying to answer it and then moving beyond trying. Getting stuck and perseverating on why abuse occurred, without coming to a resolution, can become dysfunctional. It can be difficult for therapists who have themselves moved beyond asking the why of abuse, either about their own or others' experiences, to comfortably tolerate a client's involvement in this search, but it is important that therapists find a way to do that. Furthermore, therapists should continually assess where their clients are in this process and allow each to move when she is ready. Although some clinicians might interpret this stance as avoidance of important issues or feelings, we believe it is often a stage in the process that clients will approach when they are ready. In all ten of the women we spoke with, we see resiliency in how, even at the time of the initial interviews, they had succeeded in not getting stuck. They either answered this question to their own satisfaction or let go of it.

Spirituality

We were interested in what our participants had to say about the role of spiritual belief and observance in their lives, in their healing, and particularly in the way they came to understand their abusive histories. That interest stemmed from the knowledge that many Americans describe themselves as observant and as believing in God. Some literature suggests that a strong religious faith can help people come to terms with awful life events; for example

Gina Higgins (1994) has a rich discussion of the centrality of spirituality to her resilient survivors.

To our surprise, at the time of the initial interview only half of our participants were actively involved in religion and religious institutions. To varying degrees, those five found the religious context helpful in their recovery process, although only one, Helen, used a religious framework to help make meaning of her abusive experiences. Here we give examples from several who did describe their religiosity in a positive way; then we discuss briefly what we heard from those who did not.

Elena was perhaps the most confident about the importance of religion to her. She had been raised in an observant, conservative Jewish home in which the family kept kosher and went to services regularly. She moved away from this in her adolescence but as an adult found herself drawn back into Jewish observance. At the time of the interviews, she and her partner were lighting Friday night candles regularly and carrying out more Jewish rituals at home; they were active members in a Havurah, which is a small, non-temple-based religious group, usually without a formal leader or rabbi.

Elena told us that her religion and her faith had become very important to her. "Our feeling that we are very blessed and that God is very active in our lives is present every day," she commented. Elena related a powerful story about how she "brought God into the healing." She described one Friday night when she was feeling triggered, overwhelmed, and desperately alone:

> It was a night when I was feeling particularly lonely and afraid, afraid to open my heart up again. Afraid to be hurt. So it was one of those nights, making a deal with God, "If you'll help me not to be afraid and open my heart, I'll go to services Saturday morning." . . . And I felt like my heart let go and opened up. And I went to services. And I continued to go to services for years, a cou-

ple of years. And felt very safe and comfortable and very glad I was there, that it was the right thing to be doing.

For Elena, finding God in this way and coming to terms with her abusive history were closely linked. At least part of the connection is that she had come to realize and accept that she was not alone and that it was important for her not to be alone—first most directly in her recovery and then more broadly in her life.

So for Elena, religious belief and practice played a major role in her recovery and in helping her find a framework for understanding herself in the world. It is interesting that she did not use the religious framework to conclude that there was a purpose in the abuse. Rather, the pain and need arising from the abuse helped lead her return to a relationship with God.

Psychotherapy has traditionally been inhospitable to religious belief and observance, but some therapists are realizing what an important source of strength it is for many clients and are finding ways to integrate it into their therapeutic work. Demonstrating interest in a client's religious beliefs and practices is one way to encourage him or her to talk about them and to consider religion or spirituality a possibly important factor in their healing. Therapists should be attentive to ambivalence in survivors who associate religion with family and familial abuse. At the same time, they may need help disentangling from a linkage between their spiritual leanings and abusive childhood experiences.

A number of the women in our study were significantly less involved in organized religion at the time of the initial interviews, but all had been raised in observant families, and all emphasized the importance of spirituality in their current lives. For example, Janet was not part of a formal religious structure. She came from a Catholic family—an environment she described to us as bigoted—and she had unpleasant associations with Catholicism. She associated what she felt was the bigotry and hypocrisy of her abusive parents with

Catholicism and rejected the religion as she rejected her parents' way of life.

Darlene also had difficulties with the church. She described herself as a nonpracticing Baptist. She said, "I just have some conflicts with the church and my sexual orientation so I dropped out." Felicia, another black lesbian woman raised with a significant emphasis on spirituality and religion, also struggled with the church's beliefs and practices about lesbianism. It is unfortunate that these women felt they could not turn to the church for support and community because of their sexual orientation.

Several participants described finding a useful and healing spiritual orientation from their involvement in self-help groups such as AA and Overeaters Anonymous. A few of the women who moved away from traditional religions in adulthood had been disappointed in the lack of support or acceptance from their churches. Their religions had failed them in some way, and therapists need to attend carefully to their own beliefs and values in being responsive to these clients.

We are impressed by the extent to which our participants found that aspects of their religion, particularly spirituality, can be vital to recovery from trauma, as with other terrible life events. However, listening to our participants reminds us that religion is no panacea, that it is not always right for all survivors, and that not all religious communities can provide the necessary tolerance, acceptance, and support for individuals struggling with issues of childhood abuse.

Altruism

Sometimes abuse survivors are seen negatively by the culture, as damaged, helpless, and unable to care for themselves, much less for others. That does not fit our observations of survivors, particularly not the participants in this study. We see altruism as a significant component of their psychological makeup and of their actions in the world. Steven and Sybil Wolin (1993) write about resilient survivors of troubled families having "an informed conscience that extends their wish for a good personal life to all of humankind" (p. 6), and that is how we perceived the women we interviewed.

Altruism is a complicated concept that philosophers, psychologists, and others have considered.[1] Although our participants never used the word *altruistic* to refer to themselves, many talked about the importance of doing good for others. Often they were explicit about their need to find a way to use their early experiences to bring some benefit to the world if their own world was to have meaning. Judith Herman (1992) has labeled this the "human survival mission" that is essential for many survivors' recovery.

Here we describe what they told us about the ways they have behaved that we see as altruistic. Strikingly, a number of them began behaving in such a way in childhood, and we begin with those stories.

Altruism in Childhood

Several participants told us about what we see as altruism in their childhoods. An example was this story told by Anne:

> Even when I was a very small child, I would always want to take care of littler children. When anybody came to visit, the other kids would be off playing, I would be taking care of little children. I've always loved babies, and one of my fantasies growing up was I always thought I wanted to have an orphanage. I read some book about someone in Korea who had an orphanage with all these children. And I wanted to save them all, all abandoned children.

Felicia's story is a little more complicated because her way of helping someone else involved violence, but it still has the ring of altruism. She talked about getting into a physical fight to protect a friend: "The last fight I had was when I went to camp, and I beat up this girl because she was bothering a friend of mine. And she was bigger than her and was bullying her." Similarly, although she did not want to tell her mother about the abuse that was happening to her because she was frightened of the aftermath, she finally did so when she realized another young girl was at risk from the same man. "I would think, I got to do something. And that's what made me tell my mother."

In these and other stories, we hear how their empathic ability in childhood led the women to take actions to try to protect others more vulnerable than themselves. Many survivors become exquisitely attuned to the peril of others and, given their histories, they are unable to stand idly by and let others be similarly hurt. Therapists can help clients' self-esteem by helping them recognize their capacity for compassion and altruism.

Altruism in Adulthood

Most of our participants' adult lives were shaped by their need to be of service, particularly to find ways to use their painful histories to help others in similar circumstances. Here we discuss how the need to give to others was central to their choice of careers and to career-related activities, how their reaching out to others outside of career contexts, and finally how they framed their participation in this research. Throughout, we were impressed with these women's clarity about how they benefitted from their altruism; we saw very little self-deception on this issue.

Altruism in Career-Related Activities

A number of our participants had gone into psychology or social work and were directly working with people who had been hurt or traumatized in some way. Carrie, who had a master's in psychology and thought she would probably get her doctorate, was articulate about the importance of finding ways to use her past experiences to help others and could detail some of the benefits to herself of the work:

Mostly it's very gratifying. I feel like I've learned a number of things in trying to cope with this process of dealing with all the memories and feelings that have come up. And I feel like I can really understand, I can really hear them. I can empathize with their feelings, and I feel I can give them some guideposts, constructive suggestions and things like that. I think that really, honestly, in my work, that helping other people was a way of helping myself somehow.

Carrie is interesting because she found herself trying to help abuse survivors before she remembered her own abuse. She told about a college paper she wrote, long before she had any conscious memories of abuse, describing a plan for a workshop for mental health providers who work with abuse survivors. She explained that she had thought of that topic "because in my work I've found that a lot of people who are really just in denial [laughs], or that some of the providers that I work with didn't have a lot of knowledge about this stuff." So Carrie, who herself was in denial of her history, was already struggling with learning more and helping other people know more.

We have seen this numerous times in resilient survivors. Before they have any conscious awareness of what is drawing them to the work, they find a context in which to help others that also makes it possible for them to eventually remember and heal from their own traumas. We consider this almost a litmus test for resiliency. Therapists need to help survivors see and appreciate the knowledge in themselves that enabled them to follow a path to recovery, even if they had no conscious knowledge of why they needed to do it. Learning to trust their intuition is an important step toward recovery.

Carrie knew she needed to make use of her experiences of being traumatized and then recovering from abuse in her career. "I will both try to prevent these kinds of things from happening to other people and work with people who have had this happen. And try to learn from this experience to be more helpful to other people. . . . I think that this is a part of who I am and that somehow in creating meaningful work or in making meaning in my life, that somehow I'm going to have to turn this around. If life gives you lemons, you've got to make lemonade."

Another way our participants talked about making meaning through work was to use their painful experiences as a basis for understanding and empathizing with the pain of others. Their understanding and empathy was something positive that came from their traumatic experiences and could be used to help others who have gone through the negative experience of abuse. Darlene said, "I've learned, out of this, really positive ways of how to interact with people and do therapy with other clients who've had these experiences. And I can see my history and my past continuing to help pad that base of empathy with other people because I really have been there."

These women were clear in the interviews that their traumatic histories and the aftereffects are a burden they will always carry. Acknowledging this, their resiliency was powerfully exhibited in their finding ways to make use of something positive in their experience to facilitate and enrich their careers without being "pollyanna about it," in Anne's words, and to use this to help others and themselves. Finding something positive in the abuse was enabling these women to reconstruct meaning in their lives—meaning that had been previously shattered by abuse. One way therapists can support their clients' resiliency is to help them see the strengths in the paths they have chosen and, for those who have not yet found such means of expressing what they have gained from their traumatic experiences, to help them find similar paths in their careers or in other aspects of their lives.

For many survivors, finding a way to nurture something positive from their negative experiences reinforces their sense of their own resilience. Therapists should be careful in the way they frame such observations with clients. There is something inauthentic and invalidating in simply saying, "Look at what you gained from these terrible experiences." However, helping a client see the ways in which *she herself* has transformed the negative into the positive can be a useful observation of *her power* to create something positive in her own life in spite of her losses and in spite of what has been taken from her.

Altruism in Speaking Out

Almost all participants told us that they had come to value speaking up, speaking out about abuse, offering support for others who had gone through similar experiences. For different ones, this took different forms: being politically active, writing, educating others. Most common was their growing willingness to share aspects of their own experience with other people in order to be helpful to others.

Helen was passionate about her need to help others by speaking about her family and cult experiences. In a time and a culture in which there is so much disbelief about childhood abuse, especially cult abuse, she was courageously speaking up. She told us, "When I tell my story a lot of people believe me; people hear me because I'm honest and I speak from the heart. I'd like to get through to other people and let them know they are not alone."

Anne found herself describing her personal experience rather candidly to a work colleague going through similar problems. "And I thought, 'Hey, why not?'" We asked if it felt OK. We know there is often a great deal of shame and secrecy around talking about abuse. She said, "Yeah, it felt OK. It was like, this isn't hurting me anymore. This is maybe helping someone else." At another point, she said of her abusive history, "It's deepened and strengthened, *enriched* sounds kind of like the wrong word, but in a way it's added a dimension to my life that helps me understand pain."

These women were not pretending that they weren't benefitting from the way they were helping others. Anne talked about reaching out to others; she knew it was a way to comfort herself. "[But there's comfort] also in reaching out to them and trying to figure out what would be helpful or what would they need. It's sort of a cleansing feeling too; it feels good, because of your own pain you can feel someone else's pain or reach out and do something that's helpful."

Their decision to participate in the research, which they knew was likely to be painful and evocative, also stemmed from their wish to be helpful to other survivors. Ilona said, "There are other women who need to know that you don't need to end up in a mental institution. You do not need to wind up a junkie. You do not need to wind up on the streets. Here is the power of example." She told us how important it was for her that, through the research, she could "be a force for good, if you will, for change. . . . It's not just other people, that I do my share, whatever it is." Survivors do have something important to contribute to the world. Therapists can remind them of that and help them find their own way to contribute.

In part, survivors' altruism may be influenced by their difficulty seeing themselves as deserving. It is often easier for them to see someone else with a similar history as deserving of care, and as they provide that care, begin to see themselves as worthy of similar care. Feeling and demonstrating compassion for others can be a first, sometimes necessary, step in feeling compassion toward oneself.

When bad things happen, when people are traumatized by life events, the core of their narrative about their life is often shattered. In order to recover, they must find some new framework; they must revise their story. Our participants demonstrated a remarkable ability to transform the impact of senseless violence into more self-caring understandings and meaningful actions for society. We encourage therapists to help clients recognize these qualities in themselves and nurture their resilience in transforming something damaging and painful into something meaningful and life affirming.

Note

1. At times *altruism* has been defined as behavior intended to benefit others without the expectation of reward, or at least of external reward. Interestingly, Webster's *Seventh New Collegiate Dictionary*

(1965) defines it as a "regard for or devotion to the interests of others," with no requirement about whether there is any gain for the individual doing the behavior. We have no doubt that individuals who behave altruistically do gain internal, psychological rewards, whether they are feelings of self-worth, relief from guilt, a change in the meaning of the pain, or others. In our view, these internal gains in no way detract from the value and importance of such behaviors in the world.

Part IV

A Lifelong Process

Revisiting the Participants

After we had drafted the sections of the book that were primarily based on the initial interviews, we felt it was time to honor our promise to let our participants look at what we had written about them. We also wanted to hear how their lives and recovery had gone in the five to eight years since we first met with them. Other than correcting some details, occasionally asking for changes that better protected their anonymity, and in several cases asking that we change their pseudonym (which we did), the women had surprisingly few problems with what we had written. They generally felt we had represented them accurately, though some exceptions are noted later in the chapter. And although most were stirred up by reading their stories in this form, they were pleased to have participated in the research and felt they had gained something from the experience.

In this chapter we focus on the major areas of our participants' lives—work, relationships to family of origin, and the like. We describe what we learned in the follow-up interview and how it sheds light on the women's resiliency and recovery.

WORK

In the follow-up interviews many participants talked about the ways in which changes in their working lives reflected the progress they had made in their recovery. Five had high-level professional jobs—three in mental health and two in other areas; all of the others were employed.

Most were pleased with their employment and felt there had been significant improvement in that part of their lives since the previous interviews. Most had moved to a job situation that was better for them in some way—sometimes to a job that allowed more room for self-development. The few who were not in such jobs had found ways to express and develop themselves outside of work.

For example, at the time of the initial interviews, Elena had thought she would have to leave her demanding and prestigious job because it did not leave room for many parts of herself. By the time of the follow-up interview, she had instead managed to transform that workplace. She said she had watched the culture of that setting get "kinder and gentler." She felt it now "welcomes me. I no longer feel an outcast . . . And now I bring all of me. I don't compartmentalize any more, because I'm fully there. It's an amazing change!" Elena also spoke about getting better at doing her job in these last five years. "I hear better. I'm not as reactive. . . . And I can tell when I'm triggered."

Some had no improvement in their employment but were heavily involved with unpaid work that spoke to their hearts. Anne was greatly invested in writing poetry and had met with considerable success; several of her poems had been published in prestigious places. Some, but not most, of her poems were about her abusive history. She told us, "The writing certainly helps transform everything, to see things in a new way." Ilona had recently been honored for making outstanding contributions as a Big Sister, which she had been doing on a volunteer basis for many years. She was overwhelmed and deeply moved by the recognition.

Several had abusive bosses, ultimately forcing them to leave positions and go either into less interesting jobs or periods of unemployment. In one such instance, Anne recognized her situation as abusive and left it; she ended up in a much warmer, friendlier work environment and felt good about herself for leaving. Helen had a similar experience and ultimately ended up with a more interesting, challenging, and rewarding job.

Overall we see these women as continuing to show evidence of their resiliency. Some had taken difficult life circumstances and transformed them into learning situations and, ultimately, psychological victories. We hope therapists feel optimistic about these stories, as we do, and appreciate how much positive growth can occur in survivors' lives, even over a relatively brief span of time. Survivors themselves can become discouraged when they are mired in the hard work of recovery and sometimes need help remembering that people can and do change for the better.

RELATIONSHIPS

In both the initial and follow-up interviews our participants spoke of recovery as a process of changing how they related to others. Darlene reflected, "What's happened over time is that the more I get in touch with my own issues and my own garbage, the more I see the different ways they affect relationships." We heard repeatedly from our participants about how valuable it was to finally gain insight into their own contribution to difficulties in relationships.

In the follow-up interviews, a number of participants talked about the process of moving from assuming other people would hurt them to trusting others; every participant spoke of her increased ability to trust others and to get her needs met in relationships. Helen spoke for all of them when she said, "I feel closer to women than I ever could . . . I'm not isolating; I'm present when people talk to me."

Family Relationships

There had been a number of shifts in connections with family members. For one thing, some of our participants had been able to develop close and satisfying ties with at least some members of their original families. Mostly the close ties involved some, not all, members of their families and rarely included the perpetrators.

Neither Galen nor her brother had had any contact with their father for a number of years. Galen told us about having her mother's help in arranging a confrontation with her father—her major perpetrator—on a visit to her parents' home. Her father was getting older and had a chronic illness, and she said, "I really felt like before he died, I really wanted to be able to . . . face him and to tell him what he had done to me and how that had scarred me for my life." She and he had sat on her parents' porch, and she told him that. "For me it felt like I was looking evil in the eye and, like a warrior, making it disappear. It was very powerful for me to sit with him on the porch and to tell him exactly how it made me feel." With coaching from her mother, her father accepted responsibility for what he had done, said he felt badly about it, and apologized. Galen told us that somehow saying those things to her father helped her get even clearer that she did not need to be angry at her mother. That allowed her to move into a closer and more satisfying connection with her mother.

Elena had gotten increasingly close with her mother in recent years, but her father had responded minimally or not at all to her overtures. He did not respond in any way to her invitation to come to her wedding, nor did he respond to a letter asking if they might have contact. When she spoke with us, she was struggling with the belief that she had let go of her need for connection with him and the continuing pain she had about that. She concluded, with regard to her father, "My job is to make sure I'll be as OK as I can when he dies."

Helen had severed most connections with her family and had gone to some lengths to keep them from knowing where she lived. But then her father discovered which AA meeting she attended and appeared at the door as the meeting was ending. The possibility of this happening had been one of Helen's worst nightmares, but with help from friends in AA, she came through the experience well. It turned out to be a powerfully healing experience for her, as she felt how much love and support she was getting from others, and she felt her own strength in that. She told us she was looking forward to her father's doing it again "so I can tell him myself that I don't want to speak to him." Helen's capacity to make this very distressing and potentially destructive experience into a powerful opportunity to heal and grow feels to us like the essence of resiliency. And although therapists can certainly encourage survivors to work in that direction, the most important job of therapists around such events may be to point out just how resilient the client's behavior is. Survivors often need help seeing and appreciating their own strengths.

We are struck with two things about these and other stories from the last interviews. One is our participants' continued longing to have some contact with their parents, no matter how neglectful, abusive, or malevolent they had been. The second is how much some of these connections had changed since the initial contacts. Therapists should appreciate and help clients understand that whatever stance they need to take toward their family at a particular stage of recovery will look different at some other stage, and the difference will be hard to anticipate. For example, people in what appears to be a total cut-off don't always remain estranged, and seemingly comfortable connections at one stage of the work may move toward difficult or even untenable relationships at some time later in the process. This knowledge can be particularly helpful when clients are struggling with intolerable guilt about what they are doing to their family of origin by cutting off or greatly reducing contact. We suspect that many clients know what they need to do in this regard, and unless therapists have very good reasons for believing otherwise, they would do well to respect and appreciate that knowledge as coming from some resilient core in the individual.

Intimate Partners

We saw significant changes in our participants' relationships to their intimate partners. Some whose relationships had been good at the initial interviews had even better, more satisfying, more trusting ties five to eight years later.

Carrie had married the man she was seeing when we interviewed her earlier; she said they were very happy together and were planning to have children in the near future. Elena had a formal wedding with her lesbian partner after seven years of living together, and she continued to feel extremely good about their connection. She felt things were more balanced between them now. They loved spending time together. They worked hard to find ways to deal constructively with the anger that inevitably arises between couples from time to time, particularly by talking about problems as soon as they come up. Elena told us that when they get angry, they understand it is not about that particular event. She said that both of them had been wounded by words, and both were able to wound others so, "we just don't go there. We bite our tongues quickly and try to figure out what's going on." They also attended a number of women's groups and workshops together and found that enriching to them as a couple. In general, they had developed successful ways to compensate for each person's vulnerabilities.

Ilona, whose husband of many years had died shortly after the earlier interviews, had met and become involved with a man eight or nine months before the follow-up interview. She was very excited about it—amazed that it had happened again and that she felt so free to love and be loved, and to express herself without worrying about abandonment. She was delighted with the sexual freedom she felt with this man, which was a major change in her comfort with her sexuality. She said she had been definite about her boundaries and, in fact, was not sure she wanted to marry again, although she did greatly enjoy having this man in her life. Thus Ilona was in a good relationship and felt that the impact of her abusive history had much less effect on her connections than it had in the past.

All of our participants had grown in their ability to make and sustain satisfying intimate relationships. And they were generally doing well, given how difficult relationships can be for women with such histories. Inevitably they were in different places, depending on where they were in their healing, what particular vulnerabilities their histories had left them with, and where they were developmentally. Many talked about remaining difficulties in the area of sexuality, which we know to be a particularly thorny issue for recovered survivors. However, all were doing better, all were feeling hopeful, and some were feeling very good about the place they had arrived. So our message to therapists is this: *Trauma survivors' intimate relationships do improve, and, as our participants' experiences illustrate, survivors can have satisfying and whole partnerships.* Therapists need to remind themselves and their clients of this hopeful truth.

Relationships with Children

Janet, whose children were the youngest (seven and nine), said they were a lot easier now. She told us that her son, Mathew, had been diagnosed as having ADHD shortly after the earlier interviews. She had worked very hard to get him the services he needed—a special-needs preschool program and kindergarten, psychotherapy, speech therapy, a play group at school for socialization, medication—and believed they had provided the help he needed early enough. Particularly powerful for Janet was being able to see that her younger brother, her sister, and possibly her mother had all had ADHD, and for her to be able to respond to her son's difficulties in a very different way felt important and healing. In particular, she said, "Mathew is very much like my younger brother, Carl, only Mathew is being raised without all the punitive stuff." Mathew and his Uncle Carl had become very close, and it was moving to Carl to see Mathew's difficulties being handled in a caring and nonpunitive way. In one example of what seems to us unusually sensitive and responsive parenting, Janet told us that Mathew had said to her, "I hate my brain, I can't stop it!" and she told him, "This [high energy] is a gift. . . . This is something that you will be able to put your energy into anything you want to do. Like your Uncle Carl. You can do anything you put your mind to." Janet no longer worries as much about her children. "I realize that these kids are well adjusted, happy. They are not going to be traumatized the way I was."

At one point her husband had told the children that she was having a hard time "because her family didn't treat her well when she was growing up; they were very mean to her, and they hurt her a lot." Her son seemed to accept that explanation, but Rebecca, who was older, had started asking more questions. Janet felt strongly that it had helped to let the children know as much as they did know.

We are impressed with the way Janet appears to have transcended her history in important ways in dealing with her own children, even while she continued to struggle with the effects of that history on herself. She attributes her ability to be such a sensitive and responsive mother to a great deal of help from her therapist. As to telling children about a parent's abuse, we agree with Bar-On (1995) and Snider (1994) that, provided the survivor or her spouse can tell it in a calm and age-appropriate manner, it is often better for the children to be told in words than to be left with the emotional residue that inevitably swirls around a family in which one or both parents have histories of abuse. No research or clinical evidence has been published that suggests *when* it is best to tell children about such difficult issues as sexual abuse. Telling a child about a parent's abusive history is inevitably complicated. Although children may get enlisted as healers in ways that can be problematic for them, it is also likely that they will get enlisted as healers even when they have not been told about the abuse.

When we first talked with her, Beth had a very good connection with her young son Jon, even though she had limited access to him because he lived halfway across the country with his father, who had physical custody. Between interviews she relocated in order to be more a part of her eleven-year-old's world, knowing the relationship with her son's father might be difficult, which it turned out to be. Despite the significant problems this created, Beth remained a solid and loving presence in her son's life. He was doing well, achieving in school and athletics, and taking leadership positions in peer activity. At the end of the interview she said with a mixture of pride and resignation, "So I am able to give Jon a better childhood than I had, which maybe is all you can do as a parent anyway." When we asked her if she had told him about her history of abuse, she said she had told him a long time ago. She said, "We don't talk about it now, because we don't talk about much now. . . . And at some point we will be able to talk about it."

We see Beth as having had an unusually difficult set of obstacles to overcome in being the kind of parent she wanted to be for her son. Her commitment to him and her persistence despite it all seems impressive to us and will almost certainly help Jon in his efforts to integrate different sides of his own life over time. Beth's years of therapy were undoubtedly helpful to her in being the kind of parent she had become.

Anne was uncomfortable with what we had written about her relationship with her four adolescent children, feeling that we emphasized the negative and showed too little of all that was good and nice. Five years later all of her children appeared to be doing well. She had not talked much with her children about her traumatic history, feeling she did not want to burden them. We believe it will be hard for Anne's children not to carry aspects of her abusive past until she and they can have more direct and explicit conversations about the things that had happened to her.

The participant with the oldest children was Ilona, and she had found it difficult and very painful to read what we had written about her parenting from the early interview. (We salute the courage and commitment to this project she showed by allowing us to leave it in the book, despite the distress it caused her.) When she came for the follow-up, her son Michael had visited her for only the second time in sixteen years. He brought two of his sons, and the four of them had had a wonderful time getting reacquainted and seeing the area. Ilona said, "It was such a healing process for the two of us, to be able to say to my son, 'OK, Michael, I accept you as you are.'" It had given Ilona great pleasure "to be able to introduce him as my son and say, 'and these are my grandsons.' Just to be a family." She anticipated more visits now that the ice was broken.

With her daughter, Michele, she had been very close—at times too close, she told us. Sometime after the last interview she had loaned Michele and her husband a significant amount of money to deal with some debts and then got frightened and asked for it back. With help from her therapist, she realized she needed to stop enabling Michele to misuse money; eventually she was able to set and maintain firm limits. She had been frightened that this would damage what had been a crucial relationship for her but was pleased that it had not. She concluded, tearfully, "There's been a tremendous healing and a tremendous coming together between my children and myself. I think all three of us have done a huge amount of growing and learning and accepting and understanding, and it doesn't get any better than that." We are impressed that despite her awful childhood and the difficulties when her children were young, they were able to come together in the way they had.

In the follow-up, then, we see our participants continuing to work hard on their own development as mothers. They were all doing an increasingly good job with their children; the more therapy they had, the better they were able to parent. Therapists and their clients need to know that it is possible for people with histories of serious childhood abuse to do a good job raising children. They also should be mindful that such abuse histories can, and likely will, intrude into survivors' child rearing, unless, through therapy and other growth-promoting experiences, they can learn better ways of parenting than the ones they grew up with.

For clients like Ilona, who come to therapy after raising their children, therapists can help them realize the possibility of renegotiating old relationships, which can be important to both parents and adult children. When a survivor has also perpetrated overt abuse on their children, a crucial part of their own healing will be to find a way to acknowledge, with their therapist's help, what they have done and find some way to make reparations.

Friends and Other Important Nonfamily Relationships

Almost all of the women told us about improvements in their friendships. Some said they had learned to value and enjoy the friends they had had for some time, others of feeling more themselves with friends, more comfortable and relaxed.

Ilona talked about having come to recognize and value her friendships. She told us she felt more open to feeling appreciative and appreciated and was deeply moved as she found out how much she meant to her friends. Felicia, who had not felt she had friends five years before, had close friends; she also described close relationships with two young adults for whom she was godmother and mentor. She explained the change: "Because trust is hard for me, because before I just thought, 'It's not worth it, I have to protect myself.'" But now she was willing to take the risk and knew she could deal with issues if and when they arose.

Helen spoke movingly of her closer relationships to friends. She still struggled with loneliness but found "now I can talk about it, with other people who have the same feeling." Around people's responses when her father appeared, unwanted, at her AA meeting, she felt she could see who her real friends were. Besides a solid network of women friends, Anne described several women who had become mentors to her for her poetry writing. Although she did not talk much about that, we suspect it was very important for her to have people teaching her and caring about her growth in that way.

Galen had felt isolated before but at the time of the follow-up felt better connected. She said she sometimes still struggled to reach out to someone at the moment but knew there were people available to her. "I think I've become more relaxed in my friends; I've become more real or something. I guess as I've healed more, like letting myself be myself and try to express myself and not feel I'm going to be judged." She also said she felt she had become less narcissistic, more able to realize that people's reactions often had to do with what was going on inside them and little or nothing to do with her.

Overall, most participants had become better able to see and acknowledge that people cared about them and supported them; they had become more comfortable and trusting as they reached out to others. Despite some painful times, the direction of all of their development was toward better and more trusting friendships. Therapists need to help clients see their progress and carry the hope for clients, who may not be able to do it themselves, that a time will likely come when they will make friends.

PSYCHOTHERAPY

What we heard in the follow-up interview was that for a few women, individual therapy was crucial to their recovery; many had ongoing contact with an individual therapist. Others were no longer doing individual work or had begun to work with a different therapist and were exploring other alternatives to aid their recovery.

When we asked her about her work in therapy, Felicia said, "Even though I didn't get the things I needed [in childhood], now I'm able to take care of my needs and to talk about them, and if I don't have the answers, to go find the answers. . . . And I can do that in therapy. I still have to continue therapy, I still go, because I don't think I'm there, but I need to just keep doing the work that I'm doing, and I keep getting better, every year. I can see it myself now."

Felicia had had several brief voluntary hospitalizations in the years since the first interviews. She had gotten off most of her medications about two years before the follow-up interview. She was then taking Klonopin, an anti-anxiety drug, as needed. She was even managing her symptoms from her conversion disorder without medication by using techniques she had been taught such as relaxing, meditating, grounding herself, and reducing stress.

Helen's therapy had also continued to go well. She and her therapist had made some use of EMDR (eye movement desensitization response), which she thought was helpful, especially in dealing with her acute trauma from an auto accident. Three years before the follow-up (and six months after a rape by an acquaintance and immediately after visiting the area where her mother had died on the streets in a western city) she became depressed and was hospitalized for several weeks. During that hospitalization, she learned a great deal about her fragmented parts. She told us she knew she did not have DID (dissociative identity disorder, formerly multiple personality disorder), but many parts of her needed to be acknowledged. Since then, she said, "I'm more present than I ever was before those hospitalizations." She was justly proud of her "eight years, five months, one day" sobriety and continued to attend AA meetings regularly.

Several women told us about their important therapy experiences in the past five or six years, although they were not currently in treatment. Darlene had had an extremely positive experience with a black woman therapist. After three years of productive work, this therapist encouraged Darlene to try her wings without therapy. Darlene was able to negotiate a gradual termination process that left her feeling very good about herself and confident about her ability to continue to grow and develop.

Galen also had two powerful therapy experiences in the interim. She had participated in a twelve-week trauma group and found it "amazing" and very helpful. She said that afterward she felt "a significant shift" in herself. Around that time, she decided to leave her cognitively oriented individual therapist for someone who focused more on feelings and mind-body relationships—"more earthy-crunchy," she explained. She found a therapist who was more empathic and intuitive and, for the period covered by her insurance, that person was extremely helpful to her.

Galen told us that since leaving therapy, some energy had been freed up for her creativity. Her father had been a successful jazz musician who played evenings and weekends at clubs, and she had grown up around music. Galen had never wanted to learn to play the guitar because it was so associated in her mind with her father. But she knew she was a musical person, and recently it hadn't felt right to her that she was doing nothing with music. After the confrontation with her father the guitar felt more like a neutral instrument; with therapy ended, she was teaching herself how to play blues guitar and was very pleased about it.

Several of the women had done significant work in other types of healing experiences, including meditation, prayer, Reiki (a Buddhist process of hands-on healing that involves channeling energy), and transformational breath work.

Overall, then, psychotherapy continued to be an important avenue for healing, with a number of the women also making use of a variety of treatments, including support groups, couple's therapy, meditation, body work, massage, and Model Mugging. What seemed important from the initial contacts to the follow-up interviews was that many participants continued to make use of therapy over a number of years. Given that the mental health benefits provided by insurance and managed care companies have become more limited, therapists will need to work with clients on how to best use their insurance to provide psychotherapy over an extended period of time. This might mean scheduling appointments less frequently or providing care on a sliding scale.

Our participants also found diverse and nontraditional forms of treatment helpful to them, and these alternatives did not seem in any way to interfere with their individual work, as long as their therapists were comfortable with what they were doing. Just as therapists need to encourage trauma clients to get involved in groups and in couple's therapy, so should they help their clients by supporting the judicious use of other avenues for healing. Some therapists develop lists of competent, thoughtful professionals and paraprofessionals who do body work, massage, EMDR, or other kinds of related work. Generally, survivors need more than one modality of treatment over the course of their recovery, and we encourage therapists to welcome healers onto their team. No therapist, working alone, can take a survivor of serious childhood sexual abuse on her entire journey. For therapists whose clients are involved in other forms of healing, we encourage them to pay attention to what is going on, talk with their clients about it, and be prepared to consult with other professionals when that seems useful. Just as trauma clients need help integrating fragmented aspects of themselves, they also need help integrating their various treatments; they benefit a great deal when this is done.

REMEMBERING

About half of the participants said they had remembered more since the initial interviews, and they described having gotten back many details of what had occurred during the abuse. For most, the larger outline of what they remembered had not changed. As Felicia told us, "The floodgates sort of stopped." Several remembered significant new information about the abuse. Beth had been in the middle of the process of recovering memories when we met with her earlier, and shortly after that she remembered repeated molestation by an uncle. Janet remembered her older brother's joining with their father when he abused her, as well as her brother's repeated physical violence toward her when she was very young. In both cases the women said remembering the new information helped make sense of their story. Not surprisingly, Galen had more memories when she did the twelve-week structured trauma group.

Felicia gave us a wonderful example of a piece of memory returning and then using her new knowledge and skill to deal with it. Her twenty-one-year-old godson was standing in the doorway of her kitchen eating, and it triggered a flashback of her abuser standing in her babysitter's doorway, nibbling food and planning how he was going to get Felicia away to abuse her.

And I didn't yell at him because I knew what was going on. So at the time I said, "Why don't you go sit down and eat [laughs]." And he did. And then I took a deep breath, because I don't burden him with what happened, and I said to myself, "Felicia, it's not that, it's [name] whom you love. [name], he's your godson." And I said, "Now, you're not back at the house." I just grounded myself with love. But my heart was pounding.

Given the recent focus on how and why memories return, as well as on the accuracy of "recovered" memories, we found it interesting to examine what the women told us about their continued remembering and what it meant for them. Many were in the later stages of recovery, and the new memories mostly fleshed out details of their experiences—often details that helped them understand their current reactions more clearly. Generally, they found this information valuable. We felt that neither they nor their therapists were focusing on the recovery of memories when they did return, which seems appropriate.

SELF-CARE

In the follow-up interviews these women's increased capacity to take good care of themselves was a central theme. Here we briefly describe what our participants told us in each of the major domains of self-care, including maintenance of physical, emotional, and relational boundaries, care of the physical self, and leisure.

Boundaries

At the follow-up interviews several participants told us that they protected themselves emotionally by carefully screening what they allowed themselves to watch or read. Felicia's ability to take care of herself was first manifest in her politely declining to preview the manuscript. When we asked her about it later, she told us, "I can pick up on pain so bad, I have to be careful reading other people's stories." Elena, who found it difficult and triggering to read our manuscript, said she no longer reads books about survivors and is extremely careful about what movies she watches. "Can't yet create enough distance to know it's not me, so I don't," she explained.

Many told striking examples of setting boundaries with members of their family. Beth said she had been learning to focus on what she needed for herself instead of always putting her son's needs first. She felt, as do we, that this was appropriate, especially as Jon was now an adolescent and more able to meet his own needs.

Helen's refusal to talk with her father when he appeared after her AA meeting is an example of boundary setting. Several people tried to get her to talk with her father, saying maybe he needed to put some closure on what had happened. She said she told one of them, "You know what? I don't give a flying fuck what my father needs! That's not what *I* need. I have closure on it!" She told us an example of a different kind of self-care around an emotional boundary when she said she had stopped going to church. "When I started feeling guilty about not going is when I stopped going. I don't need guilt anymore, you know, and that's not what God wants from me, either."

A number of participants told of taking care of themselves by setting boundaries at work; when that was not sufficient to create a good working environment, they got out. Anne was proud that she had been healthy enough to leave a job in which her boss continued to be abusive and harassing. Felicia's choice of a career as a freelance photographer, which allowed her to work flexible hours, was one important way she was reducing stress in her life and taking care of all aspects of herself. She told us, "I've learned to take care of myself and not feel guilty about it and not feel bad. I'm not the sacrificial lamb anymore, for a family or anyone. I have to take care of Felicia first. And I promised myself that."

Care of Their Physical Bodies

By the time of the follow-up interviews, all of these women were taking good care of their bodies. A few stories illustrate this care. Janet's energy work and Reiki were focused on her body but calmed and centered her emotionally. She also had learned to notice when her migraine headaches were coming on; she could listen to her body and slow down, which helped a lot.

Galen told about having gotten quite sick with chemical sensitivities that she thought were triggered by working where many people smoked. Her asthma worsened, and as a result of using so much of a physician-prescribed inhalant, she developed systemic candida. Eventually she found her way to an alternative doctor; acupuncture and Chinese herbs both helped significantly. She said that experience "really led me down the path of becoming even more active in my life to take better care of myself." She had become careful about what she ate and drank, but the effect was larger than diet. "I think part of that has really been empowering to me, too, in terms of my taking care of myself."

Leisure

We did not ask participants specifically about leisure activities, but Darlene's words are important and probably represent other participants as well. She said that after she had completed her doctoral training, she "did have time to engage in social activities, films, walks, talks, fun with friends. And that became something I enjoyed very much. And I've kept that an active part of my life." She also noticed that, as she moved to a city with a much higher percentage of African Americans, "my ability to meet and socialize with other African Americans and African American professionals in particular has increased, and that is something I enjoy very much, which has led to a much more positive and enriched life in terms of my cultural sense of self and in terms of the availability of events, activities, and places that are much more diverse and are geared toward African American people or people of African descent."

All of the women had become more able to set and maintain boundaries around themselves; in that and many other ways, all had become more skillful and successful at self-care. This felt to us and to them like a centerpiece of their recovery. We suggest that therapists periodically remind their clients how far they have come in learning to take care of themselves and what a triumph this is over their abusive histories.

MAKING SENSE OF THE ABUSE

At the follow-up interviews none of the women felt that they were to blame for what had happened to them, and they were not focused on blaming their perpetrator(s). They had moved beyond the question of *why* the abuse had occurred and were focused on how to live their lives. Many saw their life's work as focused on serving others and doing so in a way that made use of the hard lessons they had learned from their childhoods. Sometimes this life work was reflected in their careers, sometimes in other ways. For example, Helen told us, "I think that I went through it, made it through it, so that I could help other people get through it and know that they're not bad."

Finding the Meaning of Abuse

Darlene said she realized the abuse itself had no meaning; it was just a "negative, violent aspect of my past. . . . At this point in my life, the meanings that I've constructed have taken on a much more positive tone. I find myself having much greater sympathy with victims of violence, survivors of all types of abuse, individuals who are at risk. . . . Some people say, 'That which doesn't kill you makes you stronger.' In some ways I feel that is true in my situation. And I'm glad of that."

When we first spoke with her, Elena thought her calling was to be an advocate for people who were hurt, to speak publicly. At the follow-up we saw that her path had led in a somewhat different direction. She was providing emotional and spiritual support for people in her life to a marked degree and was also speaking her own truth, which she believed made it possible for others to speak their truths.

Even more than for other clients, trauma survivors need to find a core of meaning for their lives, and that meaning must somehow be related to their difficult histories. Therapists need to take seriously their role in making survivors aware of this need and helping them explore paths for meaning making for themselves.

Using Spirituality

At the time of the follow-up, every participant told about the centrality of their spiritual beliefs, although only a few were involved in traditional religious communities and religious practice. For example, spirituality and religion were central to the life Elena and her partner had developed; we described earlier the importance of her relationship and conversations with God. Those continued to be a core of her understanding and healing. She described learning during her breath work that she had left her body every time she was molested, and came to believe that, even as a young child, "I didn't want to be in this body on this plane in this life. And so I was looking for excuses to get out of my body. And so in the most cosmic way the molesters served me in that they gave me the excuses to get out of my body." After leaving her body a number of times during the breath work, she told us she made a deal with God to stay in her body. She said God told her that she had work to do in this life on this planet. " 'You will always be my daughter, you will always be a child of God, but you can't live there.' So I agreed during one of those sessions to that. That I can come visit and chat, and do all of those things, but that I will stay in this body and do this work." That experience and conversation changed her sense of her abuse and allowed her to reach a degree of forgiveness she had not felt before. While the concepts and language that Elena used to describe this aspect of her healing may be foreign to some therapists, we think it is important to underline how helpful this framework has been to Elena in her healing and encourage therapists to find ways to support and honor such work.

Several of the women who had not emphasized spirituality in the initial interviews told us how important it had been, and continued to be, for them. Darlene told us at the follow-up that religion had been very important to her in childhood:

> Currently I have renewed my spiritual connection with God, and often commune and talk to God, and also question God about what I feel are denigrating violent negative images that are contained in the Bible. I no longer look at the Bible in terms of absolutes, and I think this has allowed me to regain a sense of spiritual connection and again start to read and study the Bible. However, I don't actively participate in any religious activities that take place inside of a church.

We see enormous growth and strength in Darlene's having found her way back to her spirituality in a way that made room for all of who she had come to be.

Ilona told us how central the spirituality she had learned in Overeaters Anonymous had been to her. She said her spirituality is living the twelve steps in the tradition of the program, being the best person she can be, and trying to do unto others as she would have them do unto her. "Formality, no. Spirituality, yes, very definitely from the very bottom of my soul to the very top."

For Janet, spirituality was an important part of her survival and her healing. "As a child I did feel a presence with me. I used to even make room in my chair for an angel. I felt like I had some presence there that was helping me. To this day it's part of what helps me heal."

So most of these women viewed spirituality as crucial to their strength, their resiliency, and their continued recovery. Psychotherapists and others working with survivors need to know about this powerful resource and respect its importance, whatever their own beliefs and practices might be.

WHERE ARE THEY NOW?

All of these women were significantly changed from when we had seen them previously. Even though things had not always gone smoothly, and some had had setbacks, they were all doing much better at the follow-up. They described themselves—and appeared to be—calmer, happier, more centered, more at peace. They told us that they did not think often about their abusive pasts and felt that the past had less impact on their lives than it once had.

Elena is a good example. When we talked with her earlier, she had just emerged from an intense period of healing and was "creeping out of my shell to see if it was really safe to be in the world." She thought she was in transition then, "from surviving to living. Now I'm thriving." At another point she said, "I have a lot more love for everybody. I still get angry and all those things, but I have a lot more love and compassion than I used to be able to have. And it's nice." She concluded that all of her healing was "God's love flowing through me. And it's a great job to have, you know, on my good days!"

Similarly, Felicia said, "I think I've come a long way. I think I've matured a lot. I've had to get through understanding how neglect, abuse, and all of the things that happened to me affect me now as an adult. It affects all my life. It affects my relationships. It affects my work. It affects a lot of things. But I'm learning how not just to respond from old survival ways, to know that's the old way to respond. So I'm changing how I can improve myself, not be a captive of ghosts of the past."

So despite some pessimism in the field that has suggested that people with serious childhood sexual abuse tend to have more difficulties as time passes, in our sample, over the relatively short period of five to eight years, they were all doing better.

As we have said throughout this book, resilient adaptation is not characterized by an absence of pain. Some women emphasized this point more than others, but their stories revealed that all of them struggled some of the time with intense psychological pain related to their trauma histories. We saw, as some of them did as well, that the presence of pain was not a sign of the absence of resiliency.

Although in the later interviews their emphasis was mostly on sharing with us how well things had gone for them, they also told us or showed us the ways they all continued to struggle with the residue of their histories. Beth was most explicit and probably was feeling it more than some because life circumstances had made the past years so difficult. She complained that, in what we had written before, we hadn't represented how hard it is to be resilient:

> Some days it's an every-step effort. . . . In my case as a survivor I am engaged in a struggle that I don't see my nonsurvivor friends having to do. There is this constant juxtaposition of your reaction based on past experience, which is what you learned about yourself in therapy, versus more healthy ways of dealing with life. And I deal with that every single day of my life. And I'm getting much better at it, and it's much more automatic, but it's always an effort.

Janet said, "The other thing I'm accepting is that this process is ongoing. I thought, 'When I'm in my forties, it'll be done.' I said that to my husband. I said, 'Don't worry, this will all be behind me when I'm in my forties' [laughs]. And the fact that I'm getting more memories. . . . And it just made me think, I think there's even more.

So it makes me accept that this process is ongoing. There really isn't an endpoint. But the more I get out, the better I do end up feeling."

We agree that healing is an ongoing process and that all of these women will continue to deal with issues. Part of the depth and richness they bring to their lives is their continuing struggle against pain and despair. But more important are the healthy ways they find to represent that struggle in their mostly satisfying and full lives.

Appendix: Research Methodology

A detailed description of our process of developing and carrying out this project can be found in Grossman, Kruger, and Moore (1999). The decision to conduct a qualitative study was based on our commitment to providing a place for the voices of the research participants and, at the same time, allow a more holistic description than quantitative methods yield.

In order to find women for the study who evidenced resiliency, we sought people who either considered themselves resilient or were described in that way by their therapist or someone who knew them. Volunteers responded to advertisements placed around the community, for example on bulletin boards of mental health clinics and women's bookstores, or were nominated by their therapists, to whom we had mailed brief descriptions of the study and requests for research participants. One participant nominated a friend, who also participated in the study. Every participant was paid $10 per hour.

In response to our advertisements, twenty-six people called to talk about participating. An over-the-phone screening reduced that number to ten—the ten women whose stories are the heart of this book. About half of those not invited to participate were at an early stage in their recovery, and in most instances they agreed with our concern about whether the interview process would be safe and comfortable for them. Several others were not invited because we wanted our participants to represent varied backgrounds. The ten women we did interview were diverse in terms of age, ethnicity, type of serious sexual abuse, social class, religion, and other life circumstances. Two members of the research team interviewed each participant, over two or three meetings, for a total of five to ten hours. All interviews were tape recorded and then transcribed.

We used a series of interview measures, assessing each person's current life adaptation and symptomatology, history of abuse and other trauma, and methods of coping. Current life adaptation was measured by the Subjective Life Adaptation Questionnaire (developed for this project), and symptoms were measured by the Effects Checklist (Blume, 1990). Sexual abuse was measured by a modification of Diane Russell's abuse interview (Russell, 1986) and physical abuse by the Physical Abuse Scale, developed for this study. Methods of coping were explored by the Resiliency Interview, designed for this study. Copies of the measures can be obtained by writing Frances K. Grossman, Department of Psychology, 64 Cummington Street, Boston, MA 02215.

The participants ranged in age from twenty-four to sixty at the time of the first interview. Eight were Caucasian, two African American. Eight had completed college, four had advanced degrees. Their backgrounds ranged from lower class to upper middle class, and their economic status varied from impoverished to wealthy. Several had high-status, well-paid jobs; one was on disability insurance because of sequelae of her trauma. Several were in mental health work. At the time of the interviews, three were married, two were divorced, three were in committed lesbian relationships, and one was in a committed heterosexual relationship. Four of the women had children.

The voluminous transcripts, typically running three hundred doubled-spaced typed pages, were analyzed using HyperRESEARCH, a computer program for coding qualitative data (HyperRESEARCH, 1992). Using Glaser and Strauss's (1967) grounded theory approach to analyzing transcripts, elaborated by Charmatz (1983, 1990), we ended up exploring twenty-six variables, which captured most of what we considered important in the data and all of which we were able to clearly and operationally define. That meant that we could code the data with reasonable agreement. Of the twenty-six, most were content variables such as mother, father, abuse, memory, feelings, or work. Several categories referred to important processes of resiliency. These included meaning making, self-care, and self-awareness. We deliberately focused on health and strengths rather than psychopathology. Thus, for example, we did not score symptomatology. The literature is replete with examples of the evidence of emotional disturbance of survivors of abuse. For some important codes, such as meaning making, after the initial coding, we recoded at a more refined level to break the material down into small enough units for meaningful description. We worked in pairs, with each pair having responsibility for coding one participant on all twenty-six variables, generated from years of discussion.

We were mindful of the risks of what has been called vicarious traumatization (McCann & Pearlman, 1990), when researchers or clinicians working with traumatic material themselves begin to manifest symptoms of trauma. We understood such effects could distort our findings, as well as harm us, so we developed models of talking about our reactions to the participants' stories and feelings; sometimes we told parts of our own stories in order to support each other through the process. (Our process is discussed at length in Grossman, Kruger, & Moore, 1999).

We were committed to maintaining diversity among members of the research team, as well among the research participants, and were largely successful in both endeavors.

Although the project we describe seems to have developed in a linear and orderly fashion, this study, as with most other research projects we know, grew by fits and starts, like Topsy, as our understanding developed. Important issues were revisited periodically, stimulated either by input from the research community or by experiences within the group, and each time our perspective changed slightly because of our experiences carrying out the research and telling others about it. Throughout the study, certain values guided us. These include the importance of a research methodology that gives voice to those we study. Another is the importance of shifting the lens from an exclusive focus on psychopathology and weakness to a more balanced view, one that takes seriously individuals' strengths and capacity to grow in the face of adversity but does not deny survivors' pain. Another strongly held belief is that we, and others who learn from our research, have much to gain from having a diverse group of researchers studying a diverse population.

References

Baldwin, A., Baldwin, C., Kasser, T., Zax, M., Sameroff, A., & Seifer, R. (1993). Contextual risk and resiliency during late adolescence. *Development and Psychopathology, 5*, 741–761.

Bar-On, D. (1995). *Fear and hope: Three generations of the Holocaust.* Cambridge: Harvard University Press.

Bass, E., & Davis, L. (1988). *The courage to heal.* New York: Harper & Row.

Beardslee, W. R. (1989). The role of self-understanding in resilient individuals: The development of a perspective. *American Journal of Orthopsychiatry, 59*(2), 266–278.

Blizzard, R. A., & Bluhm, A. M. (1994). Attachment to the abuser: Integrating object-relations and trauma theory in treatment of abuse survivors. *Psychotherapy, 31*, 383–390.

Blume, E. S. (1990). *Secret survivors: Uncovering incest and its aftereffects in women.* New York: Wiley.

Brown, D., Sheflin, A., & Hammond, D. C. (1996), *Memory, trauma treatment and the law.* Hillsdale, NJ: Erlbaum.

Burt, M. R., & Katz, B. L. (1987). Dimensions of recovery from rape: Focus on growth outcomes. *Journal of Interpersonal Violence, 2*, 57–81.

Charmatz, K. (1983). The grounded theory method: An explication and interpretation. In R. M. Emerson (Ed.), *Contemporary field research* (pp. 109–127). Boston: Little, Brown.

Charmatz, K. (1990). Discovering chronic illness: Using grounded theory. *Social Science & Medicine, 30*(11), 1161–1172.

Cohler, B. J. (1991). The life story and the study of resilience and response to adversity. *Journal of Narrative and Life History, 1*, 169–200.

Cole, P. M., & Putnam, F. W. (1992). Effect of incest on self and social functioning: A developmental psychology perspective. *Journal of Consulting and Clinical Psychology, 60*, 174–184.

Courtois, C. A. (1988). *Healing the incest wound: Adult survivors in therapy*. New York: W. B. Norton.

Danieli, Y. (1994a). As survivors age, Part 1. *Clinical Quarterly*, 4(1), 1–17.

Danieli, Y. (1994b). As survivors age, Part 2. *Clinical Quarterly*, 4(2), 20–24.

Elliott, D. M. (1994). Impaired object relations in professional women molested as children. *Psychotherapy*, 31, 79–96.

Feinauer, L. L., & Stuart, D. A. (1996). Blame and resilience in women sexually abused as children. *The American Journal of Family Therapy*, 24, 31–40.

Felsman, J. K., & Vaillant, G. E. (1987). Resilient children adults: A 40-year study. *Advances, Institute for the Advancement of Health*, 4(4), 45–61.

Flach, F. (1988). *Resilience: Discovering a new strength at times of stress*. New York: Fawcett Columbine (Ballantine).

Floyd, C. (1996). Achieving despite the odds: A study of resilience among a group of African American high school seniors. *Journal of Negro Education*, 65, 181–189.

Garmezy, N. (1993). Children in poverty: Resilience despite risk. *Psychiatry*, 56, 27–136.

Gilligan, C., Lyons, N. P., & Hammer, T. J. (Eds.). (1990). *Making connections: The relational worlds of adolescent girls at Emma Willard School*. Cambridge, MA: Harvard University Press.

Glaser, B. G., & Strauss, A. L. (1967). *The discovery of grounded theory: Strategies for qualitative research*. New York: Aldine de Gruyter.

Goldstein, J. (1998). The role of therapy in women's resiliency: For women with and without histories of childhood abuse. Unpublished doctoral dissertation, Boston University.

Goleman, D. (1996). *Emotional intelligence*. New York: Bantam Books.

Grossman, F. K., Kruger, L-M, & Moore, R. P. (1999). Reflections on a feminist research project: Subjectivity and the wish for intimacy and equality, *Psychology of Women Quarterly*.

Harvey, M. R. (1996). An ecological view of psychological trauma and trauma recovery. *Journal of Traumatic Stress Studies*, 9(1), 3–23.

Harvey, J. H., Orbuch, T. L., Chwalisz, K. D., & Garwood, G. (1991). Coping with sexual assault: The roles of account-making and confiding. *Journal of Traumatic Stress Studies*, 4, 515–530.

Herman, J. (1992). *Trauma and recovery*. New York: Basic Books.

Herman, J., Russell, D., & Trocki, K. (1986). Long-term effects of incestuous abuse in childhood. *American Journal of Psychiatry*, 143(10), 1293–1296.

Higgins, G. O. (1994). *Resilient adults: Overcoming a cruel past*. San Francisco: Jossey-Bass.

Howard, D. E. (1996). Searching for resilience among African-American youth exposed to community violence: Theoretical issues. *Journal of Adolescent Health*, 18, 254–262.

Hudgins, K. (in press). Experiential psychodrama with sexual trauma. In L. Greenberg, G. A. Lietaer, & J. Watson (Eds.), *Experiential psychotherapy: Theoretical formulations and differential treatment approaches.* New York: Guilford.

Hudgins, K., & Toscani, F. (1998). *The therapeutic spiral: Healing sexual abuse with experiential therapy.* New York: Guilford.

HyperRESEARCH (1992). Research Ware, Inc., Randolph, MA.

Janoff-Bulman, R. (1989). Assumptive worlds and the stress of traumatic events: Applications of the schema construct. *Social Cognition, 7*(2), 113–136

Janoff-Bulman, R. (1992). *Shattered assumptions: Toward a new psychology of trauma.* New York: Free Press.

Kaufman, C., Grunebaum, H., Cohler, B., & Gamer, E. (1979). Superkids: Competent children of schizophrenic mothers. *American Journal of Psychiatry, 136,* 1398–1402.

Linehan, M. (1993). *Cognitive-behavioral treatment of borderline personality disorder.* New York: Guilford.

Lyons, J. A. (1991). Strategies for assessing the potential for positive adjustment following trauma. *Journal of Traumatic Stress, 4*(1), 93–111.

Masten, A. S., & Coatsworth, J. D. (1998). The development of competence in favorable and unfavorable environments: Lessons from research on successful children. *American Psychologist, 53*(1998), 205–220.

McCann, I. L., & Pearlman, L. A. (1990). Vicarious traumatization: A framework for understanding the psychological effects of working with victims. *Journal of Traumatic Stress Studies, 3*(1), 131–149.

McCann, I. L., & Pearlman, L. A. (1993). *Psychological trauma and the adult survivor: Theory, therapy, and transformation.* New York: Bruner/Mazel.

Mrazek, P., & Mrazek, D. A. (1987). Resilience in child maltreatment victims: A conceptual exploration. *Child Abuse and Neglect, 11,* 357–366.

Murphy, L. B., & Moriarty, A. E. (1976). The development of a vulnerable but resilient child. In *Vulnerability, coping, and growth* (pp. 295–333). New Haven: Yale University Press.

Newberger, C. M., & de Vos, E. (1988). Abuse and victimization: A life-span developmental perspective. *American Journal of Orthopsychiatry, 58,* 505–511.

Olio, K. A., & Cornell, W. F. (1993). The therapeutic relationship as the foundation for treatment with adult survivors of sexual abuse. *Psychotherapy, 30*(3), 512–522.

Pennebaker, J. W. (Ed.). (1995). *Emotion, disclosure, and health.* American Psychological Association: Washington, DC.

Pennebaker, J. W. (1997). Writing about emotional experiences as a therapeutic process. *Psychological Science, 8*(3), 162–166.

Rogers, M. L. (1995). Factors influencing recall of childhood sexual abuse. *Journal of Traumatic Stress, 8,* 691–716.

Russell, D.E.H. (1986). *The secret trauma: Incest in the lives of girls and women.* New York: Basic Books.

Rutter, M. (1985). Resilience in the face of adversity: Protective factors and resistance to psychiatric disorder. *British Journal of Psychiatry, 147,* 598–611.

Rutter, M. (1987). Psychological resilience and protective mechanisms. *American Journal of Orthopsychiatry, 57*(3), 316–331.

Sanford, L. T. (1992). *Strong at the broken places.* New York: Avon Books.

Silver, R. L., Boon., C., & Stone, M. H. (1983). Search for meaning in misfortune: Making sense of incest. *Journal of Social Issues, 39,* 81–101.

Snider, F. L. (1994). Holocaust trauma and imagery: The systemic transmission into the second generation. In M. P. Mirkin (Ed.), *The Social and Political Contexts of Family Therapy,* (pp. 307–329). Boston: Allyn & Bacon.

Starr, R. H., MacLean, D. J., & Keating, D. (1991). Life-span developmental outcomes of child maltreatment. In R. H. Starr & D. A. Wolfe (Eds.), *Child abuse and neglect: Issues and research.* New York: Guilford, 1991.

Taylor, S. E. (1983). Adjustment to threatening events. *American Psychologist, 38,* 1161–1171.

Tedeschi, R. G., & Calhoun, L. H. (1995). *Trauma and transformation: Growing in the aftermath of suffering.* New York: Sage.

Thompson, R. A., & Calkins, S. D. (1996). The double-edged sword: Emotional regulation for children at risk. *Development and Psychopathology, 8,* 163–182.

van der Kolk, B. A., & Fisler, R. E. (1994). Child abuse and neglect and the loss of self-regulation. *Bulletin of the Menninger Clinic, 58,* 145–168.

van der Kolk, B. A., McFarlane, A. C., & Weisaeth, L. (1996). *Traumatic stress: The effects of overwhelming experience on mind, body, and society.* New York: Guilford.

van der Kolk, B. A., van der Hart, O., & Marmar, C. R. (1996). Dissociation and information processing in posttraumatic stress disorder. In B. A. Van der Kolk, A. C. McFarlane, & L. Weisaeth (Eds.), *Traumatic stress: The effects of overwhelming experience on mind, body, and society* (pp. 303–327). New York: Guilford.

Webster's Seventh New Collegiate Dictionary. (1965). Chicago: G & C. Merriam Co.

Werner, E. E., & Smith, R. S. (1979). An epidemiological perspective on some antecedents and consequences of childhood mental health problems and learning disabilities: A report from the Kauai longitudinal study. *Journal of the American Academy of Child Psychiatry, 18*(2), 292–306.

Wilson, M. (1994). *Crossing the boundary: Black women survive incest.* Seattle: Seal Press.

Wolin, S. J., & Wolin, S. (1993). *The resilient self: How survivors of troubled families rise above adversity.* New York: Villard Books.

Wortman, C. (1983). Coping with victimization: Conclusions and implications for future research. *Journal of Social Issues, 39*(2), 195–221.

Yehuda, R., Kahana, B., Schmeidler, J., Steven, S. M., and others. (1995). Impact of cumulative life time trauma and recent stresses on current posttraumatic stress disorder symptoms of Holocaust survivors. *American Journal of Psychiatry, 152,* 1815–1818.

About the Authors

FRANCES K. GROSSMAN is a professor in the Department of Psychology at Boston University. She earned her B.A. degree (1961) in psychology at Oberlin College and her M.S. (1963) and Ph.D. (1965) degrees in clinical psychology at Yale University. Before coming to Boston University in 1969, she was an assistant professor at Yale.

Grossman specializes in treating adults who were traumatized in childhood. That specialty, as well as her long-standing interest in resiliency in children and adults, led her to this project on resiliency in adult survivors of childhood sexual abuse. She has authored a number of articles and chapters, including such topics as fathering, feminist research, and resiliency. She has written two others books: *Brothers and Sisters of Retarded Children* (Syracuse University Press, 1971) and (with Eichler, Winickoff, and Associates) *Pregnancy, Birth, and Parenthood: A Study of the Adaptations of Mothers, Fathers, and Babies* (Jossey-Bass, 1980).

She has been a member of the American Psychological Association (APA) and the American Association of University Professors (AAUP) since 1966. She was awarded the Diplomate in Clinical Psychology in 1970 and became a fellow in the Massachusetts Psychological Association that same year. Grossman won the Massachusetts Psychological Association Career Contribution Award in April of 1991. She was elected a fellow of the APA and of Division 35 (of the APA) in 1991, then of Division 12 in 1994. She has been a member of the International Society for Traumatic Stress Studies since 1991 and of the New England Society for the Study of Dissociation since 1990. She is a member of the board of the latter group.

Grossman has a long-standing interest in ethics and has served as a member and chair of the Massachusetts Psychological Association Ethics Committee. She is also as a member of the APA Ethics Committee. She lectures and offers workshops on ethical issues in psychology.

ALEXANDRA B. COOK is the director of children's services at The Trauma Center of Arbour Health Systems. She earned her B.A. in psychology at Yale University and her M.A. and Ph.D. degrees in clinical psychology at Boston University.

Cook's research has focused on the interface between attachment and child maltreatment. Her other interests include the effects of childhood trauma on psychology and neuropsychological functioning. She has spoken at numerous conferences on the topics of trauma, attachment, and psychological testing.

SELIN S. KEPKEP is a clinical psychologist in private practice in Brookline, Massachusetts, and is in clinical practice with Tri Valley Counseling Associates in Franklin and Milford, Massachusetts. She earned her B.A. degree (1988) in psychology at the University of California, Berkeley, and her M.A. (1992) and Ph.D. degrees (1997) in clinical psychology at Boston University. She is a member of the APA and the Northeastern Society for Group Psychotherapy. Her main research activities have focused on the area of resiliency in women with histories of abuse, with special emphasis on self-care and attachment.

KARESTAN C. KOENEN is a graduate student in the clinical psychology doctoral program at Boston University and a psychology fellow at the Payne Whitney Clinic of New York Hospital. She earned her B.A. degree (1990) in economics at Wellesley College and her M.A. degree (1994) in developmental psychology at Columbia University. Before starting graduate school, she was a Peace Corps volunteer in Niger, West Africa.

Koenen's main research activities have focused on investigating how familial and environmental factors influence an individual's response to psychological trauma. She is currently co-principle investigator on a grant entitled "The Comorbidity of PTSD and Antisocial Personality Disorder," funded by the Department of Veterans Affairs. She is also the recipient of a National Research Service Award from the National Institute of Mental Health.

Koenen currently serves as student liaison for the board of trustees of the International Society for Traumatic Stress Studies. She is also a student member of the APA, the Association for the Advancement of Behavior Therapy, and the Association for Psychological Science.

Index